ONE WOMAN'S ARMY
The Commanding General of Abu Ghraib Tells Her Story

ONE WOMAN'S ARMY

The Commanding General of Abu Ghraib
Tells Her Story

GENERAL JANIS KARPINSKI
with STEVEN STRASSER

miramax books

HYPERION

NEW YORK

ISBN 1-4013-5247-2

First Edition
10 9 8 7 6 5 4 3 2 1

To my late parents, Nelson Arthur Beam
and Ruth Sorensen Beam.

To my husband George, for always being there,
for loving me, for his untiring support,
and especially for believing in me.

To Candy and Bill King, Debby and Fred Russell,
Gail and Ken Anderson, Lauris and Cindy Beam,
and Jay Beam and Joyce Darbyshire.

To Casey, my African Grey parrot and to Doc Monk.

This book is a result of years of their collective and individual support and encouragement, of countless days of their contributions in support of my choice of a military career. Each one gave me inspiration and confidence to proceed confidently in the direction of my dreams. Thank you for the laughter, the love, and the tears. This makes it all worthwhile.

CONTENTS

ONE WOMAN'S ARMY

The Commanding General of Abu Ghraib
Tells Her Story

INTRODUCTION

I WAS SEVEN YEARS OLD WHEN I discovered the treasure chest in the cedar closet of my parents' home in Rahway, New Jersey. I opened the lid quietly, aware that I was delving into some hidden corner of my family history. Inside were private letters, old documents, and a photo of a man in uniform. The photographer had taken the picture from near ground level, portraying the soldier as a towering figure of discipline and authority. In an instant, I recognized my father. I held the portrait in my hands, examining every detail of the handsome young sergeant with his medals and polished buttons, his Eisenhower jacket, and his service cap tilted so jauntily on his forehead. Buried deeper in the box was the hat itself, flat, woolen, and a rich Army brown. I put the hat on my little blonde head and stood up straight, feeling as tall and proud as my father had in the flush of victory after a great European war.

From that moment on, I was determined to grow into that uniform. In the detours I took on my way to a military career, in the unending challenges of that career, in the darkest hours at the culmination of that service, I never lost the pride that filled me that

1

day. As I serve out the last chapter of my time as a senior officer before my retirement, I have often found myself lashing out like a cornered tiger at the boardroom generals, corporate generals, and political generals who have found it so convenient to single me out as the scapegoat for prisoner abuse in Iraq and to tarnish the reputations of many honorable soldiers under my command. But I have never lost my respect for the Army as an institution. My worst days in military service have never outweighed my best. And my best days were often the ordinary ones, those filled with military courtesies, the discipline of the parade ground, the serious work of soldiering. Any day I spent with soldiers was a good day.

I believe the uniform attracted me at such a young age because it so perfectly represented the values of those times. Of course we were all Eisenhower Republicans in my family; how could we be anything else? I grew up in the '50s and '60s with two parents, three sisters and two brothers, an assortment of cats, dogs, turtles, chickens, and an occasional duck or two. Our yard nurtured a lovely garden, and peach, pear, and apple trees. My father was an engineer and deacon of the Presbyterian Church, and my mother a hospital administrator and leader of the local Republican committee. We marched on Memorial Day, waved the flag on the Fourth of July, and pledged allegiance every morning in school. Our society had given us that new experiment in independence and affluence, the suburb. We appreciated the bounty and loved our country back, unconditionally. Patriotism was not a slogan, or an issue, or a political touchstone; it was the fabric of our lives.

Our parents were winners, mainstays of what would come to be known as the Greatest Generation. Nothing was impossible for them or their children, and in my family that applied to the girls as well as the boys. I had many female role models, most of them right in my living room. My mother's battles with the Republican men over women's and family issues—such as girls' educational programs and equal pay for women—inspired me in my own showdowns with military men. My aunt Dorothy showed me a portrait in courage as she fought breast cancer without blinking until the day it took her life at age forty-three. My grandmother Elsie (my mother's mother) told me stories of women's emancipation, and I listened to every word, living history through her. My grandmother Grace told me again and again that nobody could make me feel inferior without my permission. I believed her, even after I discovered that she was quoting a Democrat, Eleanor Roosevelt. I began studying and collecting quotes from other strong women, from Katharine Hepburn to Helen Keller to Marilyn Monroe. In college I encountered an amazing teacher of contemporary literature, the first feminist and open lesbian I had ever met. She introduced me to the strength and wisdom of New York Congresswoman Bella Abzug and other women who simply would not accept second-class status in a man's world.

Eleanor Roosevelt once said, "You have to accept whatever comes and the only important thing is that you meet it with courage and with the best you have to give." If I have tried to live by any words, it is these. The challenge set before me was to build a military career as a woman, one of the first to join the Army after it had done away with the limitations of the old Women's Army Corps and opened its ranks to female soldiers as never before. I had prepared myself in a childhood spent trying to run, ride a bike, and kick a ball harder than any boy. As a youngster I managed to dig a ragged hole in the backyard before my father interrupted my determined effort to reach China through the center of the earth. And my mother plucked me from a second-storey window before I made good on my boast to the neighborhood children that I could jump to the ground unscathed. I was one sharp-tongued, abrasive girl, and thank God the Army was ready to give me discipline and maturity. In the Army, I could make a career out of training hard, jumping out of airplanes, and trying my best to compete with men on a level playing field.

And the Army taught me to command. As I rose step by step through the ranks, from platoon leader to brigadier general, I learned that real leaders achieve that status not by shouting, but by listening, not by ordering, but by doing. My husband, George, a Special Forces officer, was my model. I admired the dedication he showed toward his soldiers, the toughness of his refusal to order soldiers to do what he would not, the discipline he exhibited as he carried out his missions in the toughest corners of the world. My husband encouraged me to reach beyond the physical, mental, and emotional barriers that stood before women in the military. Find out how far you can push yourself, he told me. Find out what Janis is capable of doing. I celebrated every promotion as an opportunity to open new doors to the women coming up behind me. But I never regarded myself as a trailblazer. My goal was to accept my challenges and do my best.

The best and worst aspects of my military career came together in Iraq. I had prepared for that challenge by serving in some of the Army's toughest male precincts, earning my parachute wings and a bronze star for my role in the first Gulf War. I served for years in the Middle East, not only as a soldier but as a diplomat training young Arab women how to bear arms for their country. In Iraq, I became the first female general ever to command soldiers in a combat zone. But I also faced a crisis that ranked as the most devastating of my life—though its circumstances did not seem completely unfamiliar to a woman serving in the military. When things went wrong at the Abu Ghraib prison, nobody stood out as a more convenient target than the female general who looked so out of place from the perspective of all those male warriors. If my superiors expected me to accept their version of events and go away meekly, they made a mistake of strategic proportions. As the commander of the military police soldiers throughout Iraq, I accept my share of the responsibility for the abuses committed by some of them who worked the night shift in cellblock 1A at Abu Ghraib. But I do not accept the aspersions cast upon the great majority of soldiers who worked at Abu Ghraib and other prisons. Nor do I accept my assigned role as the sacrificial lamb of the tale.

One of my goals in this book is to give my side of the story. The abuses at Abu Ghraib were indeed an aberration. But they were not the work of a few wayward soldiers and their female leader. They were the result of conflicting orders and confused standards extending from the military commanders in Iraq all the way to the summit of civilian leadership in Washington. A year after the Abu Ghraib photographs appeared on television screens, this point hardly needs arguing. The scandal has spread from Abu Ghraib to the far corners of Iraq, Afghanistan, and Guantanamo Bay, involving military people, CIA agents, and other civilians. Anyone fighting the counterterrorist war in the Middle East had a clear mandate—to extract actionable intelligence for use against our terrorist enemies and a growing Iraqi insurgency—but only fuzzy rules of engagement. That was a recipe for "taking off the gloves" in interrogations, and almost inevitably for prisoner abuse.

But I will not let my story be confined within the walls of Abu Ghraib. Many other forces and experiences in my life defined me. My upbringing equipped me to become a soldier in the U.S. Army, and the encouragement of my family gave me the perseverance to stay on track at a time when the path for women in the military was overgrown with obstacles. I could not have stayed on that path without help. My husband, George, served as the gold standard for military men strong enough to accept women as equal partners in the service. Let this book honor George and men like him, as well as all the female soldiers who are hard at work expanding the frontiers of military service. And let it honor the women in my life, all those who filled me with their own visions. I thank them for empowering me to survive my ordeal with my pride and patriotism intact. If I have anything to offer the next generation of military women, it is because of the gifts handed down to me in my own living room.

THE PHOTOS

I RARELY FELL ASLEEP IN BAGH-
dad. I would collapse on my bunk, pass out from the heat for a few
hours, then drag myself back into consciousness in time to go for
my usual pre-dawn run. It was only 80 or 90 degrees before the sun
rose, and the smoke and the dust seemed less oppressive under
cover of darkness.

Army leaders did not seem to want me to run, but I ran anyway.
The senior warriors peeking out of their offices and seeing this Reserve general, a woman, running at 4:30 in the morning decided
they had to do something about that—or maybe it was just a coin-
cidence that they kept changing the rules. When they announced at
a briefing that personnel—women especially—were no longer authorized to run by themselves, I had to look down at my notepad
and stifle a laugh. I was thinking, Well, if this headquarters base is
secure, what difference does it make whether a man or a woman
runs alone?

Nevertheless, I saluted, and made a mental note to find a solution. My aide and my security man hated to get up so early—they

hated to run at all—but they dutifully trotted out into the darkness every morning to keep me company.

The commanders changed the rules again. Now you could run alone, but you had to carry a weapon. So I strapped on my 9mm sidearm every morning, and saw other joggers out there lugging their sidearms or M16 assault rifles.

Somebody must have complained about that, so next came the final pronouncement: Weapons were no longer necessary, but for their own protection, women could not run by themselves before 6:00 in the morning. This rule I could not abide: 0600 was two hours too late for me, unless I wanted to collapse from heat stroke. What was the Army protecting me from behind the guards and concertina wire of this secure base? My fellow soldiers? I defiantly continued my pre-dawn runs.

One morning I came back early enough to stop at the soldiers' café and check my e-mail. The guy working the night shift in the information center seemed surprised to see me.

"Where are you coming from, ma'am?" he asked.

"Running," I said.

"You see any snakes out there?" he asked.

"Snakes?"

"Oh, yes ma'am," he said, "they love to come out in the dark, because it's cooler."

Fine. After that I took a little penlight to illuminate the path in front of me, and never came across a snake—of the small, slithery kind, anyway. And I kept on running.

Take away the whistling mortar shells and the crackle of gunfire outside the gates and I might have been jogging through some kind of bizarre theme park. Camp Victory, the headquarters of Combined Joint Task Force Seven (CJTF7), the American military command in Iraq, was located in the heart of Saddamland. The facility had previously served as a hunting camp for the dictator's loyal fedayeen militiamen and a playground for his sons, Uday and Qusay. It boasted horse barns, three fishing lakes, a stocked game reserve, and grandiose architecture, including the "water palace," a gaudy monstrosity of Italian marble rising from an island on one of the lakes. The American invasion force left its own architectural refinements behind. One of our JDAM (Joint Direct Attack Munition) "smart weapons" had neatly destroyed an office where one of Saddam's sons was reported to be meeting (we missed him), leaving untouched the buildings on either side. Our troops left the hull of the JDAM in place in the rubble as a kind of calling card.

The 800th Military Police Brigade, which I commanded, had chosen a slightly less ostentatious but no more tasteful headquarters on an island in another fishing lake, accessible by a little bridge. We were a patchwork quilt of Reserve units that had come to Iraq to hold prisoners of war in the southern part of the country, near the Kuwait border. But new orders had sent our battalions to Baghdad and throughout the country to help restore the Iraqi civilian prison system—a mission the brigade never had prepared for. Working in decimated facilities with inadequate supplies and incarcerating robbers, murderers, and suspected terrorists was not in our playbook. Nor was working in a hostile-fire zone, far from the rear areas where we normally operate. But it was our job, so we did it.

Our headquarters was located at a distance from the Victory nerve center, but we preferred it out there: Other soldiers always look at military policemen (MPs) as the bad guys; that's why we like to set up where we might be a little bit farther from the flagpole, but where we're still available immediately. Our home base was in New York, so our Baghdad digs quickly became "Gotham Island" and our headquarters building "the bat cave." The structure's glass roof had come shattering down during the American invasion, but the palm tree growing in the middle of the mess had survived, leaving us with a very breezy solarium. It was austere, but it was home, at least during the war. The place had more ghosts than bats, haunted by the victims—many of them women—of Uday and Qusay, who had used the secluded resort as their sadistic love nest.

We were told to stay away from our little lake. It was full of pollution from sewage and fertilizer—and for a time our specialists worried that Saddam had hidden nerve gas or some other weapon of mass destruction under the murky waters. The crazed fish, often leaping from the water sideways or tail first, did not reassure us. The fishermen in our group sometimes caught the creatures, examined them, then tossed them back, but our best anglers could not explain their strange behavior. It was clear enough to me: By 9:00 each morning the temperature was already 120 degrees. Those fish were boiling alive.

I kept running throughout my tour in Iraq—never feeling that I could slow down, always scrambling for money, for troops, for any way to restore prisons that Saddam had emptied and allowed to be looted before the American invasion. Each of the seventeen jails and prisons I commanded had its own crisis. Abu Ghraib, the biggest and most infamous as Saddam's former palace of torture, had to crowd most of its burgeoning prison population into tents. Another facility had barred doors but no sewage; another had heat but no barred doors. We had to secure them all against the growing number of bad guys inside and the many more bad guys outside.

On January 13, 2004, I was at our compound on the border with Iran where we held members of the Mujahedin-e Khalq, the Iranian anti-government guerrillas who had been supported by Saddam. We were involved in an operation to close a loosely authorized Mujahedin radio station. Washington had ordered the operation, not wanting to inflame Iraq–Iran tensions while feelings in Iraq were as inflamed as they were.

The absurd was never very far away in our world, and in this case it came in the form of a one-star Air Force general sent over by the National Security Council to help with the operation. This guy was a fighter pilot, and as such his ego was pretty solid. He showed up very sensibly girded in protective gear. When he walked into the room, I said hello to him and suggested we get down to business. He agreed that we needed a brainstorming session. Then he looked at me and said, "Will you do me a favor?"

I said, "I don't know. What is it?"

"Would you give me your opinion?" he said. "Do you think I look too big with these vests on?"

I said, "What?"

"Well, I caught a glimpse of myself in the window while passing by," he said, "and I thought, Whoa, you have got to go on a diet."

"You're not kidding," I said.

"I'm thinking I'll take one of these vests off," he said.

"You have two vests on?" I said.

He did indeed, but his need to feel safe was giving way to his concern over any TV cameras that might be out there in one of Iraq's emptiest extremities.

We did get down to business, developed a plan, and went to work implementing it.

That night, after returning from a meeting with the Mujahedin, I decided to check my classified e-mail. There was a message from Colonel Mark Marcello, commander of one of the criminal investigation division (CID) units. It was very brief: "Ma'am, just want you to know I'm on my way in to give a preliminary brief to General Sanchez on the investigation out at Abu Ghraib. This involves the allegation of prisoner abuse and the photographs."

Prisoner abuse? Photographs? An aide looked at me closely and said, "Ma'am, are you okay?" I had lost color, and he thought I was about to keel over.

It wasn't just Marcello's words that shocked me. It was the fact that I had no idea what he was talking about. Journalists were always trying to get pictures of the prisoners, an activity that was forbidden to protect their privacy. Had some photographer finagled access to a prison and published photos of surly detainees in their orange jumpsuits on the front pages of American newspapers? Or had one of my soldiers taken the pictures, an intolerable violation of discipline?

And what was this about prisoner abuse? Whatever had happened, how had it bypassed me on its way up the chain of command? Lieutenant Colonel Jerry Phillabaum, commander of the 320th MP battalion at Abu Ghraib prison, reported directly to me. Why was I hearing from a criminal investigator, not from Phillabaum? The "Sanchez" Marcello referred to was Lieutenant General Ricardo Sanchez, commander of CJTF7. Why was this issue going straight to him? And why was I being notified while I was in a remote outpost on the Iranian border? Was somebody setting me up?

My e-mail response to Marcello was even briefer than his message: "I don't know what to say. This is the first I've heard of it."

I had to get back in the loop. I told my aides we would drive to Abu Ghraib at first light. That meant we would hit the road and traverse a region populated by Saddam's loyalists at the most dangerous time, before the Fourth Infantry Division had started its daily morning sweep for improvised explosive devices, snipers, suicide bombers, and ambushers. Our only evasive tactic was to raise a lot of dust as our little convoy of three armored Hummers raced at breakneck speed straight to the violent district 40 miles west of central Baghdad that was the location of the Abu Ghraib prison.

I had a sense of foreboding. Whatever had happened, something had gone seriously wrong. In my six-plus months in Iraq, I had put almost all my emphasis on helping my 3,400 soldiers survive and manage the flood of prisoners flowing into our facilities. I had fought for better living conditions, more supplies, decent food, well-armed forces tasked to protect our operations, and fresh personnel to take the pressure off our overworked MPs. But I had missed something. There had been some kind of breakdown at Abu Ghraib. I knew my soldiers felt double-crossed to be serving extended tours, cursed to be stationed in that hellhole, and confused by an unfamiliar mission. They were still giving me all the effort I could ask for, but had I given them enough in return—enough retraining, enough motivation, enough confidence?

It was also plain to see that the chain of command, the nerve system of any military organization, had broken down. I had come late to the 800th—after the brigade had already mobilized and deployed to the Middle East—and I had tried to play the hand I was dealt, working through the tangle of personnel problems I inherited rather than making drastic changes. I failed to accurately assess a subordinate commander's leadership abilities. The chain of command did not warn me of what was happening while I could do something about it. My fault lay not in what I knew, but in what I didn't know—and should have known.

I walked into the prison and demanded to see Lieutenant Colonel Phillabaum. He wasn't around. Neither was Colonel Thomas Pappas, commander of the 205th Military Intelligence Brigade at Abu Ghraib. These two men did not create the command confusion at the prison, but they personified it. Phillabaum reported to me and was at least nominally in charge of the MPs who supervised the prisoners. But our leaders had given overall control of the prison to Pappas and his intelligence specialists—who did not report to me—since the great majority of inmates were held not as criminals but as "security detainees" under investigation for their connections to anti-American insurgents and terrorists. There were times when many soldiers at the prison were not sure exactly who their boss was.

I ended up talking to the second echelon of soldiers, non-commissioned officers and officers, and most of them were in the dark. It turned out that the evidence of abuse had just emerged while I was at the Iranian border. Criminal investigators had arrested seven MPs on allegations of prisoner abuse and were holding them incommunicado. The sergeant in charge of the afternoon shift said criminal investigators had taken all the guards' logs, policy directives, and notes.

"What is this about photographs?" I asked him.

"Ma'am, I've heard of the photographs," he told me, "but I don't know what they're photographs of. Maybe somebody took pictures of prisoners, but we don't know anything. None of us do."

I left a message for Phillabaum to call me as soon as possible, as one of his subordinate units was responsible for confining some of the most sensitive prisoners at Abu Ghraib. He was an actual rocket scientist—a brilliant West Point graduate and in civilian life a nuclear physicist who did licensing work for a Pennsylvania lab. Phillabaum called me that night and drove the hour and ten minutes to Baghdad the next morning to meet me at my tactical operations center. I had known the chain of command in our organization was flimsy, but Phillabaum's visit showed me how disastrously weak it was—something I should have perceived much earlier.

Phillabaum had brought a stuttering problem under control as an adult, but it re-emerged when he was nervous, so I told him to relax, take it easy, just tell me what you know. He told me what I already knew in general terms: that soldiers of the 372nd MP Company, which had joined his battalion only a few weeks earlier, were under investigation for abusing Iraqi prisoners.

I demanded to know why he had not told me about the case immediately. He didn't know enough details to tell me anything, Phillabaum pleaded. In the fuzzy organization chart at Abu Ghraib, the intelligence people were really in charge, not him, and the investigation itself was under control of the criminal division, which operates independently.

If somebody was abusing prisoners in your battalion, how could you not know about it? I asked.

The soldiers could have successfully hidden their escapades, he answered. The MPs could have used miniature digital cameras, he suggested, and their supervisors wouldn't have noticed.

Do you know what kind of pictures we are talking about? I asked.

He looked down and said, "No, ma'am, I don't. Maybe they took pictures of the prisoners in the cells."

Nor, he said, did his operations officer know, or his sergeant major, or the 372nd's company commander. Nobody knew anything.

I turned to my informal network for more details. I had made friends with Catherine Dale, Sanchez's political-military adviser, a woman with brilliant academic credentials who had always been an island of good conversation at the Coalition Provisional Authority. I called her, but this time she wouldn't talk to me. Nor would Colonel Marc Warren, Sanchez's legal aide, who had always been friendly in the past.

Over the next few days, I discovered that all my information channels had dried up. It was as if anybody attached to the 800th MP Brigade had contracted bubonic plague. Several of my aides snooped around the Coalition Provisional Authority (CPA), the center of civilian government, but also came up empty. No rumors, no rumblings, nothing. I didn't like the way this was shaping up, whatever it was, but there was plenty going on that I didn't like. I chose to believe this particular matter was working its way through the proper channels, that the truth would come out, and that the people responsible would be held accountable. I couldn't have been more wrong.

• • •

ON JANUARY 23, I WENT FOR MY RUN IN THE pre-dawn darkness of Saddamland. I showered, sipped a cup of tea, and, as usual, dropped by CJTF7 headquarters to see how the war was going. It was the beginning of a typical day of ad-libbing our way through the conflagration. Gotham Island was the heartbeat of the brigade, where my staff constantly monitored our personnel strength, equipment readiness, and other vital signs. I spent most days visiting our facilities or haranguing my military and civilian colleagues to help solve our two never-ending dilemmas: How could we protect our MPs, trained as lightly armed guards, against the growing anti-American insurgency all around us? And how could we handle our expanding population of prisoners without more resources and without corresponding reinforcements for our own ranks?

The report of prisoner abuse at Abu Ghraib was on my radar screen, but I had no idea how to gauge its importance. Investigators were taking a low-key approach so far, so I did the same; I did not want to interfere or make matters worse for Phillabaum and his soldiers. I thought it was sensible to let military justice take its course. If I had the decision to make over again, I would take the same approach today.

Sanchez and his top commanders also were treading lightly. A few days earlier, Brigadier General Mark Kimmitt, the military spokesman in Baghdad, had made one public mention of allegations of detainee abuse without giving any details, adding that an investigation was in progress. My operations officer, Major Tony

Cavallaro, guessed that our commanders were testing the waters, seeing if there was much press interest in this sort of thing. (There wasn't.) Kimmitt's statement also was useful as a cover-your-ass exercise; if details of serious prisoner abuses did emerge, nobody could accuse Sanchez and his people of a cover-up.

On January 23, I had scheduled a day in Baghdad. I went to my TOC—tactical operations center—on Gotham Island and plunged into the details of the comings and goings of troops and companies, looking for ways to punch up the readiness level of my brigade. Then, on relatively short notice, Marcello of the criminal investigation division arrived in my office with a sheaf of photos. He handed them to me, and I picked up the first one.

I had a good-size office, with maps and cards from schoolkids on the walls, a leftover Christmas tree in one corner, a bookshelf with volumes on Islam and the Koran. It was very basic and, with the two windows boarded up to protect against the occasional mortar attack, very box-like. As I looked at what Marcello had handed me, the room started shrinking, the walls started closing in on me. Nobody had fogged out the details of this photo. There were two of my soldiers—Specialist Charles Graner and Private First Class Lynndie England—grinning, their thumbs up and cigarettes dangling from their mouths, standing before a pile of butts and balls: a pyramid of naked Iraqi prisoners. I was speechless. The next photo showed England holding a prisoner on a leash.

To me, the next picture was even more heartbreaking. It showed a female MP with a nineteen-year-old Iraqi woman, a detainee whom she had befriended. I had spoken to the young Iraqi woman after she was arrested for prostitution. She said through her sobs that her husband had forced her into the profession. If we had released her, her father or brothers might have killed her to uphold the family honor. So we held her in our section for women and juveniles on what amounted to humanitarian grounds. One of our female MPs had taken her under her wing, tried to boost her spirits, taught her a bit of English. But while the MP was escorting the Iraqi woman in another part of the prison one day, somebody had told the MP to lift up the teenager's shirt and expose her breasts to the camera, and the MP had complied, humiliating and betraying her friend. I will never understand why.

Marcello pulled out another picture showing a pile of prisoners surrounded by guards. The photo showed sixteen Americans standing around, far more than the seven MPs who would later be implicated. Unfortunately, the photo did not show most of their faces. "We have to rely on the people we do identify to tell us who the other ones are," Marcello told me, "and some are saying, 'I don't know,' or 'I don't remember,' or 'I'm not telling you.' We're still working on it."

After these four pictures, I said, "I don't need to see any more." But Marcello insisted, "Yes, you do. You have to see them all to best understand what we are facing." There was an Iraqi with a hood over his head and wires attached to his extremities. There was an Iraqi handcuffed to a cell door. There were more human pyramids.

Shocked though I was by the photos, I also found myself wondering: Why is he showing them to me now, ten days after briefing Sanchez? Marcello quickly gave me the answer. He informed me that after reviewing the photographs I was to report to General Sanchez's office. Everything became clear. I had been shown the pictures because Sanchez was now ready to draw me into this drama. My prior assumptions—that the abuse may have been a relatively minor incident and that the military justice system would handle the fallout—went up in smoke. And my reflexive suspicion ten days earlier, that someone was trying to set me up, was looking to be spot-on accurate.

•   •   •

THE CJTF7 COMMANDER HAD TAKEN SPACE in the former officers' club on Saddam's campgrounds. Sanchez's inner sanctum was finished in the typical Iraqi palace decor—a Napoleonic mishmash of massive chandeliers, high-relief ceilings, and scrolled furniture. The barred windows were flanked by heavy, baroque drapes, and Sanchez's desk was a kind of pink pastel. Strangely enough, given the emperor complex of its designer, the place exuded a calm, ordered normalcy compared to the rubble and chaos everywhere else in Baghdad. While Sanchez kept me waiting, my eyes wandered over these perks of power. I was especially fixated by his impressive bank of telephones, including a red hot line. Communications were terrible in Iraq: How in the heck did he get all those telephones, and did any of them really work?

When I formally reported to him, the commander said not a word. He sat at a small conference table, and I sat opposite him. He put his hand on a piece of paper, turned it toward me, and pushed it at me. It was an admonishment directed at me, dated January 17, almost a week before our meeting. The date would indicate for the record that he had acted promptly, yet he had kept it in the drawer for a week before deciding to actually spring it on me. It read:

> The 800th Military Police Brigade continues to perform in a manner that does not meet the standards set by the Army or by CJTF7. In the past 6 months, incidents have occurred that reflect a lack of clear standards, proficiency, and leadership within the brigade. As the commander, I hold you ultimately responsible for these deficiencies.
>
> The reported detainee abuse incident at the Baghdad Correctional Facility (Abu Ghraib) is the most recent example of what I am increasingly concluding is a poor leadership climate that permeates the brigade. As an immediate step, as

the senior commander in Iraq, I am directing the suspension of the platoon leader, company commander, and battalion commander of the units involved in the incident at Baghdad Correctional Facility. You will assess their fitness to occupy leadership positions and report the results of your assessment to Major General [Walter] Wojdakowski [his second in command] no later than 23 January 2004.

I admonish you to take charge of the brigade and take the corrective actions necessary to set and enforce standards. To that end, I have requested that the commander, U.S. Central Command, provide a team of experts to conduct focused training on confinement operations, with specific emphasis on the requirement to treat all persons under Coalition Forces' control with dignity and respect.

I said, "Sir, when I saw the pictures I was absolutely sickened by them. I thought I was going to throw up."

He put his hand up to stop me. "Do you have any idea what this will do to my Army?" he said.

"Sir, I can't even begin to understand what these soldiers were thinking," I replied.

Again he put up his hand. "This is unacceptable," he said.

"Sir, I have already been thinking about the words to use," I said. I did speak some Arabic. "I will go to the Arab press. I can hold a press conference," I volunteered.

"No," he said. "Absolutely not." I was not to talk to anybody about this. If journalists inquired, I was to direct them to Colonel Warren, his legal aide.

I had good relations with the Western and Arabic press. With a little help, I could have struggled through a press conference in Arabic. Reporters knew who I was. They had been out to Abu Ghraib.

We needed to tell them that there were allegations of detainee abuse, that we would investigate these claims thoroughly and keep them informed—and that they should not forget the good work we had done in putting together a prison system that was far more humane than anything under Saddam's regime.

But going public wasn't Sanchez's game. By the time of our meeting, investigators believed that they had rounded up all the photos, and that the lurid scenes might never reach the outside world. Sanchez certainly was not going to release them himself or let me apologize preemptively. Instead, I was his contingency plan. If the photos did end up in the media, I was all set up to take the fall, not him.

He had to be worrying about protecting himself. Two months earlier, he had taken away authority over Abu Ghraib (but not the other prisons in Iraq) from me, and given it to his own intelligence officer, Brigadier General Barbara Fast, who acted through Colonel Pappas, the intelligence man on the scene. Under pressure from Washington to increase the flow of "actionable intelligence" supporting our struggle against a growing Iraqi insurgency, he had effectively cut me out of that loop and had taken direct control. But now that things were going sour, he was starting to stake down a sacrificial lamb. I didn't leave my meeting with Sanchez chastened. I was furious.

Right outside of Sanchez's office I ran into his legal aide, Colonel Warren. The commander did not listen to a word I said, I told Warren. Was there any chance of really talking with him about this? "Well, he's pretty mad," Warren said.

Usually an admonishment lists specific faults and the corrections a superior expects to see. But this single sheet spoke only vaguely of "a poor leadership climate" and "incidents" that had occurred "in the past 6 months." I had assumed command only six

months earlier. In all that time, nobody had criticized me, coun-
seled me, or blasted an email to Kuwait or back to the States about
my performance—no superior had even formally rated me. Now
suddenly I'm handed this admonishment. "Should I address my response to you?" I asked Warren.

"You don't have any right to respond," he replied.

And I said, "Well, I'm going to respond anyway."

"We won't accept it," he said. He had obviously thought this
through in advance. Since the admonishment was technically an administrative memorandum that would not end up in my record, I had
no formal right to respond.

"So what are you admonishing me for?" I demanded. "This says,
'I admonish you to take charge of the brigade.' Well, I've been in
charge of the brigade, as broken as it is, for the last six months. I've
been begging for the tools I need to do the job right, and I've been
turned away every time. What else would you like me to do?"

"He needs a couple of days to cool off," Warren said.

I did get one concession. The admonishment had demanded my
assessment of Abu Ghraib's top officers on the day I received it. Warren said I could have until the next day. I thanked him very much.

I summoned Battalion Commander Phillabaum, the company
commanders, the operations sergeant major, and first sergeants from
the battalion and military police company to my office the next
morning so I could speak to each one in my attempt to reach a fair assessment. Phillabaum appeared defeated. He and the others I interviewed still insisted they knew nothing about the photographs,
though I found that hard to believe. I completed my assessments,
most of them negative, and made an appointment for late that afternoon with Wojdakowski, who expressed only cursory interest in my
work. Of course, Sanchez had already suspended Pappas, the seven

MPs, and the military intelligence officer in charge of the cellblock where the abuses occurred. I had no opportunity to talk to the MPs involved, who already had been investigated and would eventually be charged with prisoner abuse and other offenses. In short, the process was a joke; I never heard another word about the so-called urgent assessments. Nor did anything come of Sanchez's request for a "team of experts" to train us to handle prisoners more humanely. It was the third such request Sanchez had submitted, and we had yet to receive any type of assistance. We had already had visits from two teams—both of which concluded that we had too many responsibilities and too few people to do the job. The new team would have had a tough time training us, since, as Sanchez well knew, we were transferring our authority in two weeks to our replacement brigades.

When I had a chance, I put in a call to my soul mate and husband, George, who had known me since I was in high school and had joined the Army with me. Now he was a lieutenant colonel serving with the U.S. Special Forces in Oman—and having a hard time making sense of what his wife was telling him.

"George, there's this investigation," I blurted out, "and there are these photos, and these soldiers did these things . . ." A female officer can never afford to show her emotions, but a wife can, and my tears started to flow.

"Hold on a second," George said. "When was the last time you got some sleep, because you really aren't making any sense. What photographs?"

I managed to tell my story of seeing the photos and facing Sanchez. George kept me focused on the details: the provenance of the photos, Sanchez's order to shut up about them, the written admonishment.

"This is bullshit," George said. "Who's setting you up?" He said he would get a read on the incident through diplomatic channels and get back to me.

A couple of days later he called back: There was nothing at all about Abu Ghraib in the diplomatic channels. "I smell a cover-up," George said. "They're looking for somebody to pin this on, and that's you if they can get away with it."

That dried my tears and took me off the defensive once and for all. So far, I could now see, the process had served its real purpose: to deflect blame from Sanchez. He kept the Abu Ghraib scandal buried for three more months. Then when CBS broke the story in April, complete with vivid pictures, the blame was shunted off on me. I was suspended from my command, and Sanchez remained on track for his fourth star.

I take nothing away from the accomplishments of General Ricardo Sanchez, a man who rose from his family's poverty to lead America's troops with grit and determination in one of their most difficult missions. I was proud to attach my brigade to his command.

What I resent is being scapegoated for the mess at Abu Ghraib. After more than twenty-five years as an officer in America's military service, I am still the expendable woman in this man's Army. At a time of transition for our Army, when its ranks are thinning as its obligations around the world are expanding, I am still the mere Reservist with the effrontery to seek a place in the regular Army's battle space. Nothing sticks in my craw more than Sanchez's comment during our meeting, "Do you have any idea what this will do to my Army?" There was nothing subtle about that message. This was *his* Army.

I wrote this book to dispute that claim. It is the record of a difficult, sometimes humiliating, often exhilarating transition not just for me, but for all women who have stepped beyond the velvet bounds of the old Women's Army Corps and are determined to stand shoulder to shoulder with men in an Army that needs us all. It has been a long climb, and there are still a lot of men who do not acknowledge our passage, but let me help them out. Let me state the theme of my story very clearly: It's *my* Army, too.

SADDAM'S TORTURE PALACE

IF IRAQ UNDER SADDAM HUSSEIN was hell, then Abu Ghraib was the furnace. When I arrived in Baghdad in June 2003, my assignment was to help rebuild the national prison system from rubble, and Abu Ghraib was our biggest challenge. I loathed the old prison from the moment I saw it. But Iraq's corrections system was in shambles, and we urgently needed facilities where the country's run-of-the-mill criminals—murderers, robbers, rapists, and the like—could be confined humanely and professionally. Until Iraqis could be recruited and trained, our military policemen had to act as the prison wardens and guards, jobs that were completely new to them.

Our transportation, our safety, virtually all of our support depended on the good graces of CJTF7, our mother battle station. But the warriors of CJTF7 had other priorities. They were desperately trying to root out a fast-growing anti-American insurgency before it could disrupt our plans for a free Iraq. Likewise, the civilians at the Coalition Provisional Authority, who were charged with rebuilding the prisons, had to devote most of their energies to restoring basic services like power and water. As a consequence, we ranked high on nobody's agenda. I often felt like Sergeant Bilko, trying to keep his trucks running with safety pins and rubber bands.

We knew the prison system in Iraq was in ruins. And we knew where we were most vulnerable. Of all the ghosts in Baghdad, none wailed louder than those at Abu Ghraib. Saddam had used the prison as his all-purpose repository for critics and criminals. Just about any Iraqi who was arrested—for robbing a bank, stealing a car, or defacing a presidential portrait—ended up held as a political prisoner for the convenience of his jailors. As such, he had no rights or hope of release while authorities built their case, sought bribes from his family to let him go—or simply eliminated him. Abu Ghraib was not the only hellhole, but it was the biggest and most infamous of them all. At the peak of its infamy, Saddam's regime held up to 100,000 prisoners there, nearly ten times the prison's holding capacity. The place had a thriving economy of corruption. Families who failed to bribe authorities to release their members could at least bribe the guards to smuggle in food, water, or clean clothes. Around major holidays, the dark hallways became a crowded bazaar of family visitors waving money and guards taking bribes like so many carnival vendors.

Cells built for twelve or fourteen prisoners held more than 100 in Saddam's day. "How did you sleep?" I asked one former prisoner.

"We had to divide," he said. "One-third would stand, one-third would sit, and one-third would sleep. But you didn't have to worry. You could sleep standing up, because you couldn't fall over."

There was one putrid toilet per cell and no shower for prisoners anywhere. The guards who worked there were almost as hard to recruit in Saddam's day as they were in ours, because to any Iraqi, on either side of a cell door, Abu Ghraib was a place of death. All those entering the prison had to leave their humanity at the door, and that would apply on our watch as well as Saddam's. I asked the former prisoner why it was so difficult to find Iraqi guards to take our well-paying jobs. He just shook his head. No good man wants to care for "bad people," he explained. "They're criminals. Why should you treat them the right way? They shouldn't have showers, they shouldn't have recreation. They're bad people."

If you were an Iraqi on the wrong side of the law, nothing good could happen to you at Abu Ghraib. Saddam's psychopathic elder son, Uday, would often remedy overcrowding at the prison by arbitrarily signing hundreds of execution orders. Our troops found a dozen torture cells, six on each side of a dim hallway. Their walls were covered by the scribbling of condemned prisoners: "These are my last words on this earth," or, "I am going to Allah." Within earshot of the torture center were the hanging chambers, each with two nooses positioned over iron trapdoors. When the hangman pulled the big lever, the iron doors would slam open against the concrete siding of the vault below, giving the torture victims a noisy harbinger of their own final journey. Our guide to these facilities mentioned "gas rooms," and we assumed he was talking about gas for heat until he said, "No, no. If the rope didn't kill them, they would take them next door and gas them."

The prison's hospital wing was a fossil from the Dark Ages. Some of the medical people did have a gentler approach, we were told: They administered truth serum rather than beatings. But in rooms near the hospital we found cruder implements for prying information from the inmates: an iron cage that could be fastened over a prisoner's head, a chair with straps around the seat, hooks in the ceiling where prisoners in hand irons would dangle for as long as a day or two. Saddam's medical "research" was designed to test the limits of human endurance: How much torture could a prisoner take and still be able to talk?

Abu Ghraib was only the most prominent of the Saddam family's prison playgrounds. Uday was particularly fond of the country's main women's facility in Baghdad. He would select a young woman from the inmates, have her brought to his office at Iraq's Olympics organization, which he headed, and rape her repeatedly. American troops found numerous bodies buried nearby as well as a tree near Uday's office where he would hang some of his victims naked rather than simply shooting them. A rare survivor said that when Uday tired of her, his henchmen hoisted her into the tree by her neck. But she managed to keep breathing, feign death, and finally escape.

America's invasion plans interrupted such atrocities. In November 2002, months before our divisions marched north from Kuwait, Saddam could see the war coming. In order to spread chaos, he opened Iraq's prison doors and released every last robber and rapist into the streets. The only exceptions, we believe, were inmates at secret political prisons, who were simply shot. The prisons didn't stand empty and unguarded for long. Iraqis quickly descended on them, ripping out windows, doors, copper wiring, plumbing fixtures—anything of any conceivable worth. In one wing at Abu Ghraib, looters ripped out every last cell door, leaving them in stacks along the wall as if planning to come back for them later.

When the Third Infantry Division, the Marines, and other American forces descended on Baghdad in March 2003, they found Abu Ghraib in ruins. Ordinary Iraqis and international humanitarian groups regarded the place as the epitome of evil, and would happily have ground the rubble into dust and sown the ruins with salt. But the 18th MP Brigade, a regular Army combat support unit that arrived with the infantry, couldn't ignore the benefits of the 20-foot wall that still surrounded the prison, mostly intact except for a northern section. With the addition of a few strands of concertina wire, a couple of land mines, and some government procured tents, the MPs threw together a temporary holding area for Iraqi prisoners of war. There was no electricity or running water, but at night a half-dozen generators provided light. The 72nd MP Company, a National Guard unit out of Henderson, Nevada, was put in charge, holding up to 200 prisoners at a time for three or four days until they could be shipped south to our main enemy prisoner of war (EPW) facility at Camp Bucca, near the Kuwait border.

When I visited Abu Ghraib for the first time, scouting potential prison facilities in July 2003, my reaction was visceral: You gotta be kidding. We drove west along the main supply route from Baghdad. The prison gate, about 100 yards off the road, was all but unreachable. Our most experienced driver tried to navigate the rubble and concrete, ruts, and ditches that blocked our way, past the crater where a roadside bomb had blown the rear wheels off a 5-ton truck. We finally gave up and walked the last few yards, assured that the mines had been cleared. The dynamic young company commander in charge, Captain Todd Armstrong, was all fired up, offering me a "tour of the prison facility" as we stood together in ankle-deep debris.

"Do I have any prison facilities here?" I asked him.

"We will," he assured me, "or that's the plan."

As I looked around, all I saw were building walls apparently knocked apart by sledge hammers, gaping holes where windows and doors once had been. In the hallways, the rubble became knee deep.

"I can reasonably envision this working," Armstrong said.

"Well, you've got a wild imagination," I responded. "I don't see anything we can do but level this place."

"We're only going to use it to the extent we have to," Armstrong said. "This is no place to run a prison."

We could certainly agree on that one point.

My conviction grew stronger as Armstrong showed me the torture and hanging chambers. The 18th Brigade had taken human-rights groups on the same tour, and they had been adamantly opposed to using Abu Ghraib in any capacity—likening the idea to

turning Auschwitz back into an operational prison camp. When the
Coalition Provisional Authority's prison department started floating
the idea of using Abu Ghraib as a temporary facility while a new
prison was being constructed, the humanitarian groups—as well as
the U.S. State Department—expressed almost violent opposition.
Sandy Hutchinson, a State Department representative, told us to get
all the prisoners out of Abu Ghraib as soon as possible, then close
the place down.

To make matters worse, Abu Ghraib was in a horrible neighborhood. The prison was organized as a big north–south rectangle,
about 2 miles long and encompassing 60 acres bounded by those
20-foot walls and dozens of acres outside of the walls. The community around the prison—the town of Abu Ghraib itself—was a
wasp's nest of anti-U.S. sentiment. If the people to the north were
unfriendly, occasionally lobbing a mortar or firing a rocket-propelled
grenade (RPG) to let us know of their displeasure, the Iraqis to the
west—a neighborhood we called "Little Mogadishu"—had even
more violent anti-coalition feelings. To the east stretched the road to
Baghdad, never a secure area. Only to the south, where the prisoners
had farmed vegetables and livestock before the land was taken over
by squatters, did the neighbors seem to tolerate U.S. forces.

The second time I visited Abu Ghraib, insurgents lobbed in a
mortar shell to greet me. I climbed one of the guard towers, scanned
the horizon, and could see nothing that looked like hope. A few buildings were still standing—warehouses, a foundry, a laundry, a metal-
working shop, a textile factory, and the mill where Uday used to
thrust in prisoners' arms, grinding them off up to their elbows.

Baghdad's new civilian overlords wanted to see the place for
themselves and came to visit on July 12. I briefed Sergio Vieira de
Mello, head of the UN mission in Iraq, and L. Paul Bremer, head of
the Coalition Provisional Authority, then showed them around Abu

Ghraib. De Mello in particular asked probing questions about whether Saddam's torture prison might have a role in a more civilized regime. I told the visitors it was not a good location for a prison operation at all. Under our rules, prisoners ideally are held in safe areas far behind the lines. Abu Ghraib, by contrast, sat in a hot zone, along a dangerous road between Baghdad and the rebellious Sunni Triangle. Small-arms fire peppered our positions several days a week. Several nights a week we were hit by mortars and RPGs. As I delivered my briefing, two mortar rounds exploded on the far side of the prison wall, bouncing the rubble at our feet.

"Is it dangerous?" De Mello asked. "Should we be here?"

"This is what it's like out here," I said.

Bremer, who tended to be curt, demanded, "Why *are* we here, General?"

"This is the only facility we have right now—today—where we can hold anybody securely," I answered. "Until a new facility is built, this is the best we have."

"If this is the best we have, we're in trouble," Bremer said.

"Yes, sir, Mr. Ambassador, we are," I said. I explained that we could set up a camp on the design of an EPW compound, though the common criminals we would be confining were much more dangerous and difficult to handle than prisoners of war. I had been assured by civilians in the CPA's prisons department that a new, properly located, modern prison could be ready to occupy—or at least nearly so—within six to eight months.

"And what are they smoking?" Bremer responded.

We must have walked 20 miles around the prison grounds that day. De Mello was under pressure from the humanitarians and wanted to judge their apocalyptic claims against the reality of Abu Ghraib as he saw it. He poked his head in everywhere, talked to the engineers, and scoped out the twenty-four cellblocks we would have available if we went all out and reconstructed the whole prison. Walking through the damp, stinking corridors was not a pleasant exercise. Debris left by the looters had blocked the sewage system and raised pools of raw sewage to floor level, a putrid swamp flowing under the chunks of concrete, rebar, and twisted metal. Finally Bremer stopped me in mid-sentence. "Janis, I can't stay here any longer. I can't stand the smell," he said.

When we stepped outside, he said, "It's not much better out here." There was no cemetery as such on the prison grounds, but experts in the mass-grave inspection teams that followed the Americans into Iraq suspected that thousands of bodies were buried in the dry earth. Engineers working to clean and level the landscape stopped and meticulously collected any bones they came across. We never found the mass grave, but the whole prison smelled of death and decay.

Bremer's mind was made up before we began the tour: He knew we needed to make use of Abu Ghraib, however foul it was. I didn't want to concede that point so easily. Maybe we had no choice but to use Abu Ghraib now, but we also had to make a firm commitment to abandon the putrid torture chamber as soon as possible. De Mello seemed as reluctant as I was. "What if we use it only on an interim basis?" he suggested.

"Mr. De Mello, that's the best solution," I answered. "If we call it an interim facility, then everybody will start asking when the new one will be ready." Bremer signed off and committed funds to restore the prison as a temporary solution. We even changed the name of the place to "Interim Prison Facility, Baghdad Central." Of course, everybody continued to call it Abu Ghraib. I said good-bye to my guests, and they returned to Baghdad. A month and a week later, a truck bomb exploded under Sergio de Mello's window at the UN office in Baghdad, killing him instantly.

For all our diplomatic legerdemain, the bottom line was that Abu Ghraib was back in business. We surveyed the cellblocks, which stretched in a quarter-mile-long row beyond a huge gate closed by an iron door on rollers. We started our reclamation project in the north end of the barracks-like building, with the first cellblocks on either side of the central corridor. We were going to do it right, putting only about a dozen prisoners in each cell and equipping the cells with solid bunks and good mattresses, safe wiring and sanitary facilities. These would be our models, setting new standards for the Iraqi corrections system. We called them cellblocks 1A and 1B.

I felt plenty of foreboding about Abu Ghraib. But never could I have imagined that within four months, MPs in my brigade would turn cellblock 1A into a global symbol of human degradation and humiliation—precisely the evils we were trying to combat. These MPs also subverted the code of behavior that guides every soldier from the private to the general, whether in the regular Army, the National Guard, or the Reserves. I became a soldier simply because I loved soldiering, from the morning runs to the parade drills to the parachute jumps to service in the world's combat zones. But my career became more than the sum of my experiences. The Army enlightened me to the ideals of service and respect, and made them part of me. Those lessons of my Army career gave me the fortitude and discipline to face what happened at Abu Ghraib—and to stand up to the indignities that some of the Army's own senior generals were about to inflict on me.

ADVENTURES WITH GEORGE

I WAS BORN IN 1953 INTO A MIDDLE-class family in the middle-class city of Rahway, New Jersey. It was a racially mixed community, though the races were fairly clearly divided by St. George Avenue. We were one of those '50s families of the *Saturday Evening Post* covers: four girls, two boys, and a staunchly Republican Mom and Dad living in a happy house with all the loving grandparents nearby. On Sundays we attended the big, beautiful First Presbyterian Church, which was always crowded to the rafters, with two ministers and a full choir. (When I go back to the same church now, only thirty or forty congregants occupy the cavernous space.) I stayed near home to go to Kean College in Union, New Jersey, married my college sweetheart, then came back to Rahway to teach in the local high school. That's when I could have settled down and started building my own big family, but there was always something about me that just didn't feel comfortable in the suburbs of New Jersey.

Perhaps I had spent too much time in the company of my uncle Fred, a towering man with a handlebar mustache who could play the piano like a maestro. Fred had had two wives and numerous careers, from insurance to investments to publishing. But above all he was a traveler, regaling us children with tales of Chinese junk rides, German opera performances and the onion domes of Ukraine and Russia. Don't ever think that the place you live is the only place you can experience, Uncle Fred would say—and that world of possibilities always stayed with me.

But Uncle Fred wasn't the only adult who gave me a dream. When I was in high school, my physical education instructor, Ms. Rohanic, introduced me to the magic of teaching. She was one of those inspirational guides who encourage students to see the possibilities in their lives and to chart a path toward their goals. I really thought I wanted to be a dancer—ballet, tap, whatever—and she took that very seriously, channeling me toward a modern dance class and letting me discover my limitations on my own. In college, I majored in English and minored in secondary education. I no longer wanted to be a dancer; I wanted to be Ms. Rohanic.

I found a new mentor when I worked as a student teacher in another New Jersey town, Glen Ridge. It was 1974, and educators were experimenting with flexible "open" classrooms and techniques like the magic circle and the infamous "new math." My hero, Ms. Gisell-Baker, showed me the creative sparks of mainstreaming our students—serving the gifted and the challenged equally and simultaneously. I met some of the most fascinating kids in this setting. I will always remember the boy who could add up numbers in his head if you read them to him rapid-fire but had trouble putting them down on paper. He developed the inestimable talent of identifying Glen Ridge's passing garbage trucks by the sounds of their engines. He would shout out, "Number 23!" from his seat, which was nowhere near the window—and sure enough, if you looked outside you would see truck number 23 rumbling by.

This was where I wanted to be, but when I got my degree and

actually started teaching in 1975, there was no Ms. Rohanic around to inspire me. I taught the standard high school English course—grammar, literature, a touch of speech. I tried to find ways to make it interesting but found myself stymied by an extremely conservative school system that forced me into a narrow curriculum. Even when some of us suggested a fresh new idea for a school play, the veteran teachers and administrators would only look at us like, what? The students were as cynical as everybody else, and the curriculum was so iron-clad that the high-schoolers would say: "Oh, it's November? Time to diagram sentences. December? Get ready to start reading *War and Peace*." Maybe the parents of our students wanted it that way. After the ructions of the '60s, they wanted a calmer, more stable educational environment. They wanted me to be the traditional schoolmarm, carrying thick books in one hand and a ruler in the other. I thought of being stuck for twenty-five years in that role, producing no students who would thank me or even remember me. It was not a pleasing prospect.

When I was in college, I had found a tear card in a *Reader's Digest* and filled it out on a whim. I was asking for information about something called the Reserve Officers' Training Corps—"ROTC." An Army recruiter subsequently called me, but when I got on the phone, he said, "Oh, I should have paid more attention to your card. I thought I was going to be talking to a man." He thought "Janis" was a man's name? I remember looking at the telephone receiver in disbelief. You have women in the Army, don't you? I asked him. Yes, he said, but not many in ROTC. Besides, Kean College did not have an ROTC program at all. If I was interested, I would have to transfer to Rutgers University, but he could make no promises that I would get accepted into ROTC there. Forget the Army, I thought at the time.

But as I grew more disillusioned with teaching, the Army option started to seem attractive again. I had never joined the anti-military bandwagon of the Vietnam era. My upbringing had something to do with that. Under our roof you were either Republican or you were silent. Military service might have been completely out of fashion in the late '70s, but in my house it was still considered an honor to serve your country.

I did check out the anti-war movement once, skipping school with a friend to attend a moratorium outside the courthouse down the road in Elizabeth. I wore faded jeans and an old field jacket that I found in my father's closet. With my hair stylishly frizzy (I would braid it tightly at night and comb it out in the morning), I looked more like Janis Joplin than Janis Beam (my maiden name). The students and other people who showed up formed a peaceful crowd, even if we did look like refugees from a depression-era food line. Nobody looked very healthy, or very happy. Journalists were circulating, asking whether we used marijuana and what we thought about the Vietnam War. Even then I was hesitant to open my mouth and say anything to anyone holding a notebook or a microphone. I listened to some of the speeches, talked to some of the activists, and simply couldn't see myself in their movement.

I did start paying more attention to the war. I read *Time* and *Newsweek* and watched the evening news. Every night the newscaster would tell of the latest horrible battles and give the latest depressing body count. I thought to myself, "This is not the United States. We're better than this." Almost as dismaying was the spectacle of our veterans returning home from Vietnam to jeers and abuse. Many of their fellow Americans regarded the war they had fought as evil, and many veterans were embarrassed by their service. That seemed all wrong.

When I called the Army recruiter in 1977, this time he came right over to my apartment. In the space of a few years, the demand for women soldiers had grown. The pendulum had swung: The same Army that previously had brushed me off was now eager to have me. The Carter Administration was doing away with the outdated WACs of the Women's Army Corps—the organization of soldiers in skirts who had served behind the lines since World War II. In the new Army, women soldiers would have primarily staff roles in fields like medical services, administration, and communications. They would still be excluded from battle divisions, though they could fill a few specific office jobs at the higher corps level. But none of that diminished the significance of the new policy. For the first time, women were joining the mainstream of the U.S. Army, and their opportunities could only expand from there. Already, previously closed fields were opening up. A year earlier, the first women were admitted to West Point, 119 of them. Women could not take up arms in combat, but they could join combat-support units specializing in chemical warfare, ordinance, military intelligence, and military police. Women were needed as platoon leaders and company commanders—and would command men as well as other women. The skirts were coming off.

The status of men, of course, was part of this equation. As the Army restructured itself into a voluntary force after Vietnam, it was attracting plenty of male recruits who wanted education and training that would carry over into civilian life. But the Army also needed warriors, and there were not so many volunteers for that assignment. That's where the women came in. Our policymakers' plan over the next decade was to steadily expand the ranks of women holding jobs in combat support and combat-service support. As more women were given roles as truck drivers, supply officers, intelligence analysts, and the like, more men would find those jobs closed and be forced to join the ranks of the warriors. And once you became a professional infantryman, you were much more likely to make the Army your career. There were lots of civilian jobs for truck drivers and electronics technicians trained by the Army—but not so many for combat fighters. The Army didn't make a big deal of the fact that it was recruiting more women in order to push more men into combat, but that is what it was doing.

The recruiter had an easy time selling me on this opportunity. I accepted all the propaganda without a blink. The Army might not send me to a fascinating European assignment fresh out of basic training, but I knew I would eventually get to sample the world, from Germany's opera halls, to the deserts of Arabia, to Egypt's great pyramids, which had fascinated me since I was a schoolgirl. If I had a chance of escaping my hometown mentality, this was it.

I had a partner to go with me. Between my junior and senior years in high school, my little sister Gail and I headed for Seaside Heights, on the New Jersey shore, where I found a waitressing job. While my sister, who was only fourteen, was walking by one of the game booths—knock over the bottles, win a stuffed panda—the young man running the place started calling her. When "Blondie!" didn't work, he tried "Little Wind!" (She was so skinny that he figured a very light breeze could knock her over.) He asked the girl to fetch him a Tab with ice. That's how Gail met George Karpinski, and that's how I got my introduction.

George had served as president of his high school student council in New Jersey and had just finished his sophomore year majoring in biology on a four-year scholarship to Wittenberg University in Ohio. Like me, he had had wanderlust since he was a child—in his case, expressed through a love of long-haul trucks. Under his tutelage, I soon learned as much as I wanted to know about Peterbilts and White Freightliners, Jake Brakes, and reefers. George was used to having strong women in his life, starting with his mother, who raised him, his twin brother, and two other children after their father had died of a heart attack when the twins were eleven.

A lot of men might have been put off by my lofty fantasies of traveling the world. But George was attracted to my determination and spirit, and I saw him as my rock, the exemplar of hard work and integrity.

We corresponded and kept in touch on vacations for the next couple of years. After George graduated, he moved back to New Jersey and discovered that he loved teaching high school biology. By that time I was away at college myself, but at least we were in the same state—and I had fallen head over heels in love with the guy. During Christmas of my junior year, he asked me to marry him. I asked for time to think about it, but practical George had already won my father's permission, and I was not about to say no in any case. In November 1974, halfway through my senior year, I took two exams early, married George, drove through the West on a whirlwind honeymoon and made it back in time for my last semester.

Three years later, when I was frustrated by my own teaching experiences and exploring a military career, George encouraged me. He could find a teaching job anywhere I was stationed, he told me. But the recruiter was as interested in George as he was in me, and he sold us on a joint career. The Army had a policy of keeping married officers together. We could travel and see the world arm in arm, we were told. We should have known that was too good to be true.

Off we went to join the regular Army as officer recruits—George the model of an officer and a gentleman, and I the pioneering woman who never thought of herself as someone who was about to start a private war against military traditions. Call me naïve, but from the day I was recruited it never occurred to me that I was about to intrude on hallowed male turf, that I would have to find my place on the fringes of a man's Army. What transfixed me instead was the ex-hilaration of embarking on an adventure that people in Rahway would never have conceived of. I would learn the military arts. I would jump out of airplanes in parachutes. George and I would see the world. Joining the Army was just so cool!

Even basic training sounded exotic. I received a packet wel-coming me to Fort McClellan, Alabama, "nestled in the foothills of the Appalachian mountains." I had never been to Alabama before, but it sounded lovely. The young New York woman on the same plane, also headed for basic training, had never been there either, as she announced repeatedly throughout our journey. When our little Piedmont Airlines flight landed in Anniston, Alabama, this woman walked down to the tarmac, looked around, and asked, "Where are the redcaps? I can't possibly carry all these bags." She developed the strength very quickly. In front of a bus next to the terminal stood a female drill sergeant wearing a hat that looked as if it could slice your head off. "Recruits!" she shouted. "Get on the bus! Don't talk! Get on the bus!"

On the ride to Fort McClellan I kept gazing out the window, wondering where the foothills were. But the monotonous land-scape of that part of northern Alabama didn't lessen my excitement and eagerness for this adventure. When we arrived at the front gate, I saw them everywhere: soldiers! They were walking, running, marching in formation—they were everywhere you looked. The ser-geants took us to a long barracks and gave the officers room assign-ments. I had grown up with three sisters. Now I suddenly had 100 of them.

Many of the other recruits had seen more than I had—growing up in a place I couldn't even imagine, like Oklahoma, for example, then living in California. Some were working on their third or fourth husbands. A good share of the women seemed to be running away from something—a boyfriend in some cases. Had I joined the U.S. Army or the French Foreign Legion? I was especially impressed by Camille Yastrzemski, who had a sizable name, impressive hair, and a large personality. Camille had been in the Army before for two years, then she got out and came back in, so she knew everything. She knew all about the culture of Alabama, for example. On one free day she led some of us to a bar—probably the only bar open in Anniston, Alabama, on a Sunday afternoon. As we entered the dark and dingy establishment, the bartender, a jovial fellow with perhaps two teeth in his mouth, greeted us like his long-lost daughters. While savvy Camille tried to get him to cash a check without levying a service fee (she succeeded), I couldn't stop staring at a big open jar containing some kind of purple liquid and what looked like giant floating eyeballs. Finally the bartender grinned at me and said, "You want an aiggg?"

I excused myself for not understanding him.

"You want an aiggg?" he repeated patiently.

"No, no," I said. "What are they?"

"They're hard-boiled aigggs," he said. He reached in, plucked out one of the amazing-looking orbs with his bare hand and offered it to me on the house.

By this time, I was backing away from the bar toward a grimy wall. Camille rescued me, buying two pickles and two eggs and leading us out of there. As I emerged into the bright sunlight, all I could think was, "Oh, my God, I survived!"

Basic training was much less mysterious. Physical training (PT) and long marches didn't bother me, since I was always pretty athletic and fit. In my high school, during those days before Title IX boosted support for girls' sports, the boys had football, basketball, and baseball, and the girls didn't have much. There was a summer softball league, and in phys ed classes we played volleyball and competed in races. I took advantage of everything I could: You either liked phys ed or you hated it, and I liked it.

In our early days at Fort McClellan, we marched to the PT field wearing skirts over our shorts. That was a holdover from the WAC days: A proper woman does not march with too much leg exposed. Once at the field, we would take our skirts off, neatly fold them, and exercise in our shorts. That bizarre practice ended after about two weeks, when we began proudly marching to the field in our shorts.

I gradually started to understand more of what it was like to be a woman in the Army. Our infantry instructor, Captain Scott Hyatt, was very patient. He taught us combat tactics such as battle maneuvers, envelopment, direct attack, and defensive operations as well as more practical skills, including how to dig a foxhole and how to fire and clean a weapon. Our lessons in hand-to-hand combat would not have struck fear into the hearts of any enemy. We spent one afternoon covered in padding and hitting each other with sticks blunted by cotton batting. We might as well have been wearing those big sumo wrestler suits you can blow up, put on, then fall all over the place like an idiot, but Hyatt was patient. He expected us to absorb these lessons as well as any male soldier could. We might never use what we learned on a battlefield, but it was important for us to understand the business of the Army. If you don't know what units are facing on the battlefield, you can't effectively supply or transport them or support them in any way. Fighting skills were what I wanted to learn. It was not that I hungered to carry a rifle, go out to the battlefield, and shoot people, but you could learn how to process paperwork or organize logistics anywhere. Fighting and survival skills you could learn only as a professional soldier.

Hyatt was a veteran of Vietnam, and he told us frankly of his doubts about an expanded role for women in the Army. He pointed out that many senior women who had come up as WACs had similar doubts.

"This is our Army," he said, gesturing to include himself and all the women sitting before him. "It's changing, but it shouldn't change too much."

Some recruits raised their hands immediately and asked why, if women proved that they were capable and fit, they couldn't serve in the infantry.

Hyatt's answer was blunt. "There isn't training in this school that can prepare you for the realities of war," he told us. "You can be fit, you can be ready, and you can be a man, ladies, and you still may not be able to handle the realities of war."

There was dead silence in the classroom.

"If you think you're ready to do this, the first thing we need to decide is whether to put women and men side by side at the infantry school," he said. Then he added: "And I hope that day never comes."

No amount of Army training can override the social standards of the times, Hyatt argued. If society gave women a certain status from the day they were born, he said, the Army was not going to change that after they reached adulthood. He was suggesting, without saying as much, that women still had a protected place in America and were not prepared to take the initiative in the dirty work of war-making. And men were trained from boyhood to take care of women. If one of two men in a foxhole took a round, Hyatt said, the other typically would continue the fight until he had a chance to check on his buddy. But if a woman were wounded, her male foxhole companion would check on her first and lose his focus on the enemy, risking two lives. And if a man was wounded in that situation, Hyatt said, experience showed that much the same kind of dynamic would play out: The woman would lose focus and try to summon aid for her male counterpart.

I respected Hyatt's opinion at the time, but nearly thirty years later I believe his kind of reasoning is out of date. On a modern battlefield like Iraq or Afghanistan, without any real fronts or rear areas,

a female trucker or MP can find herself in harm's way just as suddenly and directly as an infantryman. Men and women have fought
off ambushes together and been caught in firefights together. Believe me, the instinct that dominates is not courtesy toward the opposite sex, but survival. In the Iraqi war zone I have seen women
become every bit as tough and flinty as men. It is often hard to tell
men and women apart as they work together in their desert camouflage uniforms. Hyatt was right that our society shapes the
norms of the Army. But today's society is producing women who
are stronger, faster, more athletic, better educated, and determined
to climb to the top. These are the women who will continue to play
a more important role in our armed forces—and eventually go to
infantry school with men.

•   •   •

ECHOES FROM HYATT'S INFANTRY COURSE
stayed with me throughout basic training. I was determined to become a soldier's soldier, as he was. But I had to acknowledge something else about myself: I also wanted to remain a woman. I wanted
to be tough, but not to lose my femininity. The Army was wrestling
with the same conundrum. Although the idea of basic training was
to tear down our old values and perspectives and rebuild us into
Army women, all in four months, in fact we trained in a protected
environment, isolated from the men of Fort McClellan—and from
the overwhelmingly male culture of the Army. Some of us had a
lot to unlearn. On our first trip to the field, we took equipment
like canteens, entrenching tools, and our shelter halves. (You carry
half of a tent, and your foxhole buddy carries the other half.) We
trained, raised our tents, and set up watches like proper soldiers. My
foxhole buddy, Antonia, and I pulled an hour of sentry duty at 1:00

in the morning. We awoke in our underwear and T-shirts, dressed in our uniforms, crawled out of our tents to fulfill our military assignment—and I thought I must still have been dreaming. "Toni! Toni!" I hissed. "Put your glasses on and look over there!" Sitting outside another tent, having a smoke, was a soldier dressed in baby-doll pajamas. That's when I learned that not everybody adopts the military mind-set at the same pace.

Everybody who survived the training eventually got the point. Within the first couple of weeks, our instructors took us to see battle tanks from Vietnam that were undergoing repairs at the Anniston Army Depot, near Fort McClellan. After my first look at these machines, nobody had to tell me that I had chosen a deadly serious career. Some of the women in my group treated our military instruction more nonchalantly—like those dumb required courses you have to take as a freshman. They didn't have to pay attention to all this nonsense about tanks and infantry and field artillery, they thought, because they were heading off to an administrative or medical position. If there was ever a war—in the Middle East, say— they would be stationed in Tampa or Germany.

My attitude was different: If you're an Army officer, there's no safe place in a war. I respected women like Brenda Carpenter, a member of my recruit class. She had been an enlisted soldier for seven or eight years and had to take our class to win an officer's commission. She was mature, carried herself with a military bearing, and did everything well. She ran faster than anybody in the class, she studied harder, she asked the smartest questions, and she had a plan for her future. A lot of our classmates resented her because of her intelligence, her confidence—seen by some as arrogance—and because she was one of only two or three black women in our group. But I was on friendly terms with her. We both saw not just the limitations for women in the Army, but the brighter prospects ahead.

She didn't have much respect for women who wanted to stay away from the action. "They won't always be able to hide behind the safety of a typewriter," she told me once.

All kinds of rumors circulated about Brenda—especially that she was a plant from military intelligence assigned to monitor the women's program. Eventually she failed a physical because of some kind of back problem and had to leave the Army before we graduated. I was amazed: She had looked perfectly fit to me. I remember thinking, There's always something they can use. If they don't want you, they'll find a way to get rid of you.

We all had to find our own style of leadership. Brenda would have been a leader by example. As freshly minted second lieutenants right out of basic training, we were sent to an officer orientation course to begin unraveling the mysteries of leadership. Among other things, our instructors assigned us to meet with the enlisted trainees who eventually would be following our orders. We interviewed and worked with these young female soldiers, listened to their concerns and encouraged them. I enjoyed the exercise. After the first half-dozen or so interviews, I tried to establish some kind of personal contact with each of them—an understanding that went beyond our differing ranks. And of course, I had to get used to the idea of ranks, as well. As the first young woman came in and reported to me, I was shuffling through her papers. When I finally looked up, she was still standing there rigidly with her salute in place because I had not returned it. Oh, yes, I thought, I forgot. I'm supposed to do something here.

Through much trial and error I learned a key aspect of leadership: An officer does not have to exude perfection. To get through a military career successfully, you have to maintain your poise at all times, but you also have to be able to laugh at yourself. Soldiers will respect you if they see you are not afraid of your own flaws. I tell soldiers all the time, Hey, I don't have all the answers. Soldiers have always made me smarter, so don't be afraid to give me suggestions, to tell me that we're not doing something as well as we could.

I also knew that military leadership involves more than just listening. I can never forget staring in awe at those tanks in Anniston. Those chugging, smoke-belching monsters had killed people on a foreign battleground. This is what the Army does: It fights and it kills. It wasn't the idea of killing that overwhelmed me—as cold as that sounds—it was the enormous responsibility of performing military service for my country, of leading soldiers into danger. As we rode in the tanks on a test track, you could feel the treads grinding and rattling. Guys in the armored units called them "metal caskets," and I imagined these soldiers clanking into battle in that claustrophobic, smoky, cold, loud, and awkward space. The cumbersome vehicles seemed to inch along, turning like a battleship on land. But that didn't really matter. If something got in the way, these things would blow it up or clank right through it or over it.

As I sat in that dark place, my heart pounding, I asked myself: Could I? Could I? If I were responsible for this vehicle, could I take soldiers into harm's way?

THIS WOMAN'S ARMY

READY OR NOT, AFTER MY INITIAL
training I plunged into the mainstream of the U.S. Army. I was still
on my own. George had reported to duty late because of a bout
with chicken pox and was still at men's basic training in Fort Benning, Georgia. When I moved to "the other side" of Fort McClellan,
as we called the base beyond our restricted corner, I quickly discovered the existence of a world that had totally escaped me during my
first months in "the foothills of the Appalachians."

The base's WAC culture, in particular, came into clearer focus.
In basic training an old-school lieutenant colonel had served as our
battalion commander. She had always dressed primly and appropriately, looking like a WAC recruiting poster from the '50s; you could
imagine her going to tea wearing a hat and with white gloves over
her manicured nails. She wore her hair in a bouffant style from the
same period, her little hat perched on top. Her fatigue uniform was
tailored to look as if it had been painted on her. She had the trouser
legs pegged to fit smartly inside her boots. She put herself together
meticulously. She used to stand in the orderly room and have someone slip her boots on so that she didn't wrinkle her trousers.

On the other side, I now learned about an even more impressive figure: the base commander, a larger-than-life career woman who was one of the first female two-star generals in the Army. She stood almost six feet tall, matronly and imposing, and soldiers whispered that she had a live-in woman companion. That should not have been surprising. It turned out that Fort McClellan was the Army's hotbed of lesbianism. This had somehow escaped my notice while I lived in a barracks with scores of other women in basic training. In retrospect, I realize that probably half of my classmates were lesbians. I recall one woman who kept a naked picture of herself beside her bed. At the time I thought she was eccentric, but now I understand that she probably was engaged in a little marketing. During my months there, I saw no overt lesbian activity in the barracks and nobody propositioned me, but clearly, those who were interested could have had plenty of action. Some of my classmates must have considered me the densest suburban square they had ever met, but I was shocked the first time I heard a man spit out to a woman who had angered him: "You must have been at Fort McClellan for a while, you dyke."

Dyke? I sought out my friend Judy Adams, a sergeant who had been around the Army for a while. "Is that what people think?" I asked her.

"This is Fort McClellan," she shrugged, "home of the dyke."

"Are you serious?" I said. I had had no idea.

"Sure," she said. "That's what everybody says about it."

"But it doesn't seem like that's true," I protested.

And she said, "Well, it's good that you say that, because that means you're one of the straight ones," which was her way of establishing *herself* as one of the straight ones.

How could there be any doubt that I was straight? I was married, after all. But I later discovered that in the Army, marriages of convenience were common. Two soldiers might get married simply to qualify for off-base housing and other privileges. Or a soldier might marry a civilian friend simply so that the civilian could qualify for insurance, military discounts on things like cigarettes and booze, and other benefits. A lesbian soldier I knew in Germany married a gay German man while her lover, a German woman, married his lover, an American Air Force sergeant. They all switched partners and lived happily with full spousal benefits.

In my case, the fact that I had a husband who was often absent signaled that our marriage was probably some kind of scam. That made me fair game for any number of sexual adventurers.

Fort McClellan was not a lesbian haven by chance. It had served as the main training center for female soldiers for years. In addition to providing basic indoctrination and officer orientation for women, McClellan housed the military police school and other schools open to both men and women. WACs felt that they almost owned the place, which even featured a WAC museum. If you were a service-woman, it was hard to go through your career without spending quality time at Fort McClellan. And if you were a career Army woman, chances were also better than average that you were gay. In those days the Army tended to attract women who had doubts about their femininity. If gay men had their Greenwich Village, gay women had the Army and Fort McClellan, an environment where they felt accepted, where they could form a community of solidarity with many like-minded sisters and feel safe and secure in the ranks. After my shock wore off, I accepted the reality of Fort McClellan as an aspect of the diversity I was finding and welcoming in my new military life. I was meeting people from all races, from all walks of life, from every part of the country—and with a variety of sexual preferences.

This last manifestation of diversity produced a classic don't-ask, don't-tell compromise. The Army brass obviously knew about the rampant lesbianism at the base, but nobody in the high command ever said or did anything about it. It may have been taboo for Army men to be gay, but that was not the case for Army women. In part that was because the women were discreet; there were no lurid scandals, no wild clubs outside the front gate. But another factor was that Army men, including those who ran the service, were tolerant in a condescending kind of way. Their attitude was: Of course Army women are dykes. What other kind of woman would want to dress like a soldier and play a fringe role in a man's world?

The men of Fort McClellan had their own special culture. Perhaps it was my imagination, but it seemed to me that McClellan's ambience tended to produce men who were more macho than usual. The officers' club was very popular, as were similar clubs throughout the military. Women officers as well as men were required to join as a way to keep the establishment afloat—even though they were paying for features like topless dancers on Wednesday and Friday nights. And it was really no place for a woman. Male officers gathered after work to yuk it up, slapping each other on the back and complaining about their two pet peeves. One was civilians, especially the civil servants who had taken over some of the Army's record-keeping and other tasks. In the world of these Army men, civilians were lazy, spoiled, and slovenly. "Yes, I married a civilian," a male officer would say. "That way I can fuck one over every day." Their second bugaboo was the steady advance of women in their ranks. "The biggest mistake they made was letting women into the regular army": I overheard that one all the time—often while standing in the same club as these guys.

When I finished officer orientation and moved over to the military police school at Fort McClellan, the abuse got nastier. The women admitted to MP school had to prove themselves every day.

We were training alongside men from ROTC programs, from West Point and military academies like the Citadel and the Virginia Military Institute (VMI). At first I wondered why all these men who didn't know me could be so hostile. Judy Adams helped me sort it out. These men believed that military police work should rank as a combat arms mission. In their view, allowing women into their midst diminished their status. Also, everybody comes into the MP officer program as a second lieutenant, she explained. So graduates of the prestigious academies have to establish an informal pecking order. They compete vigorously among themselves (just as they did back at their academies), but they agree on the fundamental division: Any male second lieutenant trumps any female second lieutenant.

I should add that I met many, many men in the Army who did not fit this stereotype. These were pros, like Scott Hyatt, who accepted an expanding role for women because that was the Army's policy, and these pros would try to make it work. Others came from families with strong women—a professional wife, a brilliant daughter—and had no problem giving equal status to female soldiers. I learned one of my best strategies for fighting the war of the sexes a little later in my career—from a man. I returned exasperated from a meeting, complaining that men around the table were always trying to distract me by tossing out some line like "It's nice to see women wearing skirts again." Next time that happens, my boss and mentor suggested, don't engage them on that level. Say, "Thank you very much, but now let's get back to the business at hand." I tried out the line at the next opportunity and it worked. Meetings went much more smoothly after that, with no more sidebar comments about my physical attributes.

Still, I kept on running into double standards. In Fort Bragg, an extremely quiet military intelligence officer named Fay was transferred to our unit. She was a real standout, with striking blonde hair that fell below her waist. And she was accomplished, a first lieutenant who had risen from the enlisted ranks. But her promotion also contributed to her downfall. She was accused of becoming intimately involved with a company commander, a captain who was married but separated. The man's estranged wife got wind of the affair and together with the battalion commander knocked on Fay's door at just the wrong time. She should never have let them in, but she did—and there was her lover in her quarters. She was removed from her intelligence job, sent to our MP battalion in limbo, and put through a two-year ordeal of investigations by officer-reviewing boards and the inspector general. She stayed in the Army, fought for her reputation, and retired in good standing. The captain left the Army rather than go through the same ordeal—and eventually married her. He was unlucky to fall in love with a female officer, because a male officer won't get in trouble from his involvement with just about any other category of woman. He should stay away from the enlisted ranks, but such liaisons happen all the time. You hear men say, I met my fiancée in the Army; she's getting out because she's enlisted. But unfortunately for Fay and her lover, this permissive code was trumped by the double standard that decreed, God forbid that a female officer should get caught fraternizing with a male soldier: That is cause for a major scandal.

Some women—even straight women—tried to neutralize the men by joining them, cutting their hair and playing down their female characteristics. For my part, I tried to be both an officer and a gentlewoman. Our uniform required us to keep our hair up, off the collar, but we didn't have to cut it, and I kept mine at shoulder length or longer. I was a blonde when I entered the service and I'm a blonde today (though now I need a little help to stay that way).

When I worked in the Middle East, my fair hair, green eyes, and pale skin could be a real distraction for Arab men. If I wore my hair down, men would look at me as they did the Russian prostitutes who did a thriving business in Dubai. But if I pinned my hair up, military style, men would take me seriously. I dressed conservatively in long sleeves and ankle-length skirts, and if I knew I was going to receive extraordinary attention, in Saudi Arabia, for example, I would slip on a *shayla*, the headscarf traditionally worn by Muslim women. American contractors in Saudi Arabia would say, Look at you. You've become one of them. I would answer: No, I have not. But when I go into a meeting, I don't want the subject to be my blonde hair or my legs.

In my travels around the Middle East, people would sometimes come over and touch my hair and my skin, very gently, to see if these features felt as different as they looked. In Yemen, I bent down to shake hands with a little kid and he tried to touch my eyeball. During my time in the United Arab Emirates, I would run or swim every day, and hoped that the tan I was picking up would help me blend in better. But I refused to dye my hair black, as some Western women did to stand out less conspicuously. The way to be taken seriously in a man's world is to force them to engage your intelligence, not to try to change what you are.

PLAYING WITH LITTLE GUNS

I HAD MISGIVINGS ABOUT JOIN-
ing the military police from the start. The MPs weren't sure about
me, either. The male bias of the branch was probably sharpened
by insecurity. MPs wore the "little guns," the branch insignia of
crossed pistols. An ambitious young man rocketing out of West
Point toward a general's stars wanted no part of any little guns; he
wanted the big guns—the crossed rifles of the infantry. Only after
establishing himself as an infantryman might a young officer consider transferring to the military police—positioning himself as a
big gun among the little guns, so to speak.

It cheapened the credential for all of them when women were
admitted to the branch for the first time, only a few months before
I came along. And the Army wasn't sure that its women should be
carrying weapons and arresting people. Only after the Navy included women in its shore patrol did our leaders finally accept the
idea of female MPs. Under that reform, women still were kept out
of the MP units attached to infantry divisions, for those cops directed traffic and took charge of prisoners on the battlefield. But we
could work behind the "forward edge of battle area" guarding in-

stallations, running enemy prisoner of war camps, escorting prisoners, and performing the other duties of uniformed police officers. Even that role caused some discomfort among the Army brass. An MP-qualified woman reporting to a new base often would be steered toward a softer job in something like protocol—as if she knew anything about that—after some male battalion commander decided that military policing would be too risky for her. The MP veterans themselves were still getting used to this new era when I came knocking on the door.

Taking the job seemed like a logical move at the time. During officer orientation, my platoon leader, an administrator in the adjutant general's corps, had steered me toward a position in office work or supply, the kinds of jobs that women could perform comfortably. She did mention more "aggressive" possibilities in military intelligence or military police, but she wrinkled her nose at the thought. I knew my own inclinations, and they were the same as George's. He was training to be an infantry officer, and he knew I was no pencil pusher. He urged me to work with real soldiers, people who were fired up and seriously committed to a military mission. I also took the list of possibilities to my former infantry instructor, Captain Hyatt, for his advice. He pointed me where I wanted to go, toward more soldierly jobs in communications, intelligence, or police work. He knew of my not-so-secret ambition to become a parachutist, so he focused on the military police in particular. MPs do have a wartime mission, he pointed out. They do deploy to war zones, sometimes rapidly, sometimes by parachute. Joining the MPs would give me an entrée to jump school.

The recruiter back in Rahway had shown me a videotape of shore patrol and military police officers working together, arresting criminals, but the job didn't appeal to me; for one thing, there were no women on the tape. And I couldn't see myself standing sentry at a control gate looking at drivers' licenses. But the idea of deploying to dangerous places—by parachute!—won me over. Only two other of the 101 women in my class hiked over to the MP school at Fort McClellan with me, making it the least popular branch among the women in my group. When we reported for duty in 1978, our lives improved instantly in some little ways. We moved from a barracks to a modern building with officers' billets—tiny one-bedroom apartments where you had your own kitchen and bathroom. We even had whole weekends off—an eon of free time that we could hardly imagine how to fill. When George was free, I would drive the two hours to Fort Benning to visit him. Shopping also did the trick. Once I went to the PX with Judy Adams and bought a pair of red and white Nike running shoes. "What do you need those for?" Judy asked. "It's going to be months before you have to take another PT test."

But I needed them now, I told her. I had been going out running every morning in my military shoes, and my feet needed a break.

Judy looked at me and asked, "Are you crazy?"

"I've been doing this for months," I said. "I was doing it in basic training."

"You really *are* crazy," she said.

I kept on running—down the road outside our quarters or over to the other side of the post. I never really paid attention to the mileage. I was just running. It was such a wonderful feeling of freedom—just me and the breeze. I will never forget those red running shoes. This was at a time when you rarely saw women out running. There were a lot of excuses: It's unsafe, I don't want to go by myself, I don't want my boobs bouncing up and down. That kind of talk sounds strange today, but in the 1970s athletics and physical exertion were still largely a male domain. In basic training and MP school, our physical training requirements were more lenient than men's. We did push-ups on our knees, not our toes. We were exempted from other upper-body tests, including monkey bars and chin-ups. We were given seventeen minutes to earn 100 points on our 2-mile run, while the men had fifteen minutes. It was just assumed that women could not keep up physically. Women in our MP basic course developed bad backs or sore ankles, opted out of PT, and still were allowed to graduate. Men mostly just gutted it out, worked through the pain.

Give the Army credit for working to level the playing field over the years. It reduced the PT test to three events, push-ups, sit-ups, and the run. There are still different standards for each sex, but the women are catching up. Today young women come to the Army from schools that offered them a full range of athletics and urged them to keep fit. Girls are out there playing basketball, field hockey, lacrosse, soccer, and many other sports, and their models are women like Mia Hamm, who broke down a lot of walls. As a result, women's athletic skills—including upper-body skills—are improving, and running is almost a way of life.

Almost unconsciously, I made it my goal to compete with men on their level. They beat me on push-ups, but I could hold my own running and could outduel just about anybody in sit-ups. Our MP class of nearly seventy soldiers would do sit-ups until the last person stopped. Since I could do about 300 at a time, that was usually me. I didn't like having everybody gathered around me watching—I didn't want to be some kind of freak—so I usually stopped at a reasonable number instead of going for the maximum. In any case, we really couldn't win in the end: Men would always point out the easier standards for women. I gave the same response time after time. "Things are changing," I would say. "We'll see where we end up."

Without question, men who had come from the service schools or transferred from the infantry were better prepared for MP work than were women who had just finished a few months of basic training and orientation. The men could drill more smartly and show off better military skills and tactics, and they had a better grasp of the rules and regulations. A more important test for women was to show that we could lead soldiers—men and women alike. From time to time our instructors sent us out to spend a day supervising enlisted soldiers training to be MPs—the troops we would be commanding after we qualified. At the end of the day we would ask the trainees for feedback. On one occasion the Army put us female officers together with female enlistees for some frank talk on how the enlistees were being treated. Many complained they were being harassed from all sides—by fellow recruits who regarded them as "cupcakes" and by male drill sergeants who peppered them with sexual innuendos. We relayed their concerns to the Defense Department Advisory Committee on Women in the Services (DACOWITS), a civilian group that advised the Pentagon on how to recruit and retain women in the armed forces. But DACOWITS was another institution rooted in the '50s, when it was formed, and offered little relief to women facing greater challenges in the '70s.

To be a good leader, you needed self-confidence, ambition, respect for the Army as an institution—and a good sense of humor. In my first role, as a platoon leader at Fort Bragg, North Carolina, we had to prepare for possible riot-control duty in Panama around the time the United States agreed to turn over sovereignty of the canal to the Panamanians, in early 1978. Our technique was a stomp and drag. Ranks of MPs holding shields and nightsticks advance menacingly, stomping their front feet, then dragging their back feet forward. The platoon sergeant was comfortably familiar with the maneuver—he had been previously assigned to Panama—but I had practiced it only very briefly at the MP school.

"Don't worry, ma'am," the sergeant assured me, "I'm going to keep you out of trouble."

First we went through the mechanics and got rid of the glitches, the questions, and the self-conscious laughter. Then I started shouting commands through a bullhorn with the sergeant standing beside me: Shields down! Batons up! On line, march!

After a couple of run-throughs, the troops were looking really good, and my confidence was sky high. The sergeant had me face the advancing troops and march backward, while he stood behind the troops, flashing me a thumbs up. I was stomping, dragging, and shouting with gusto right up until the back of my helmeted head slammed into the tree limb. Bonk! At least I maintained enough composure to bring the formation to a halt before everybody marched into the same tree.

After I put the troops at ease, I headed for the rear of the formation and confronted the sergeant. "Why didn't you give me a warning?" I demanded.

"I wanted to see if you would recover," he said easily. "You passed the test."

In the Army, of course, passing a test means you get to go on to a tougher one.

IT'S OKAY, I CAN SUFFER

AFTER QUALIFYING AS A MILITARY police officer, I immediately went to jump school at Fort Benning, linking up with George, who was in officer candidate school. I felt like I was sneaking in through the back door. Army planners had decided that it was safe enough to assign female MPs to a corps, the umbrella group under which battle divisions were organized. I believe they overlooked the fact that a corps sometimes deploys a "jump TOC," a tactical operations center that forms part of a headquarters to the rear of a battlefield, yet potentially quite close to the action. Sometimes these TOCs actually do jump in, which requires MPs qualified as parachutists to help secure the area. It is not the same as serving at the front, but it is certainly closer than anybody had ever expected women to be.

Consciously or unconsciously in those years I took decisions that put me as close to combat as a woman could get. I wanted to be in the real Army, not in an office. I wanted to serve with professional soldiers, thanking God that the Vietnam era of dope-smoking draftees was over. I didn't want to be a pioneer or a war hero; I just wanted to acquire the skills and experience necessary for advancement in my chosen career. When a jump team from the 82nd Airborne Division put on a demonstration for us at Fort McClellan, that was all I had to see. As the paratroopers glided down with square canopies, trailing an American flag and landing precisely on target, I thought: This is something I would never do as a civilian. Maybe I still couldn't join the fabled 82nd, the "All Americans" who had been commanded by Bradley and Ridgway and jumped into North Africa, Italy, and Normandy, but as an MP I sure could learn how to jump.

At Fort Benning, there were no differing standards for women and men. I had no problem with that principle, although my knees did. During the first few days of the four-week course—"ground week"—the instructors had us practice the parachute landing fall by jumping off an 8-inch block. Over and over, we practiced the technique of collapsing our legs, rolling on our hips and shoulders, and hopping back on our feet. We listened to our instructors closely, especially after a chaplain in our squad landed off balance and broke all ten of his toes. As part of our conditioning we ran constantly in our combat boots—no red and white Nikes allowed—a brutal experience. At night, people would rub ointments on their legs and wrap them in cellophane to try to ease the pain of shin splints. My knees felt like giant balloons. I kept waiting for them to explode and burst out of my skin. By the time it was over, we all hated the word "ground."

In jump school, women who had previously resisted the idea of cutting their hair short finally did, but I held out. I liked my shoulder-length hair, the last vestige of my femininity, as far as I was concerned. You couldn't use barrettes, pins, or anything solid to keep your hair up, so I used 2-inch masking tape. I would get out of the shower, put a braid in my hair, turn it up, fold it back, and hold it in place with a length of tape. It was time-consuming, but when I returned from instruction, all it took was one rrrip!—and I had my hair back. My knees might be throbbing, my boots and baggy uniform might be filthy, but my hair was down and I was still a female human being. A female airborne sergeant who was training us couldn't understand my attitude. "Alpha Whiskey Three," she said one day, calling me by the designation on my helmet, "why don't you just cut your hair off? It will grow back." Ripping off the tape "seems pretty painful," she said.

"Sergeant Airborne," I answered, "it's okay. I can suffer the pain."

They say every jump you make during initial training is a night jump because you do it with your eyes closed. That's normal, they told us. You should be afraid. I did have my eyes shut when I went out the door for the first time but quickly opened them to get my bearings. I counted off the seconds: one thousand one, one thousand two . . . If the chute didn't open by five, you had to pull your own rip chord quickly because you would be screaming toward the earth, but I felt the tug after two seconds. Then everything went into slow motion. There I was, floating in the sky. I tried to remember what I had to do. Check the canopy. Control the toggles on the right and left risers that you can use to move out of the way of other parachutists. Determine the wind direction and face into it, slowing the forward momentum of your canopy and setting you on course for a gentle landing. Then I made a rookie mistake: I looked down. Everything speeded up again and I seemed to be hurtling toward the earth at 200 miles an hour, a sensation called "ground rush." Actually, I was descending at a rate of only 5 or 10 miles an hour and managed to land smoothly. On my next jump I did it right, judging how far I was from the ground by keeping my eyes on the horizon. Sergeant Airborne made sure I got the point: "Last time I checked, ma'am, the horizon wasn't straight down," she barked.

Jump school gave me a set of parachute wings over my pocket and a strange legacy of fear and exhilaration. I've been nervous about looking down from heights ever since, but at the same time I fell in love with flying. After graduating I got the assignment I wanted— Fort Bragg, home of the 82nd Airborne. George got orders to the same base, but we were beginning to get the idea that parallel assignments would not always lead to togetherness. My husband the biology teacher had given himself the most demanding transition to military life possible. In the space of about a year he put himself through men's basic training, officer candidate school, infantry officer basic training, jump school, and finally Ranger school, joining that elite band of soldiers trained to specialize in close combat. Then, no sooner had we arrived in Fort Bragg than George went off to Special Forces school, qualifying him to join the Green Berets who often fight behind the lines or on secret missions without conventional support. When he emerged from field training in the mountains of western North Carolina he looked like a prisoner of war. He was emaciated, his head shaved, his face covered with camouflage paint, his body full of mosquito and chigger bites. He winced as I took off his shirt, baring his protruding ribs and blisters from the heavy equipment he had carried on his shoulders.

For a time after that, George was almost a stranger to me. His 12-member A-Team had to be ready to deploy anywhere in the world on 24 hours' notice. One time it might be South America, the next time the Middle East—I usually didn't know. George would get the call, race to the airport, then reappear two weeks later or two months later. Typically, my phone would ring at 2 A.M. and I would be told I could pick him up. He often would be thin and ragged, running on the dregs of nicotine and caffeine. For a few days he would still have his field mentality, chewing tobacco and cursing about "fucking this" and "fucking that." The first few times this happened,

I would challenge him, demanding, "Who are you?" But that was the wrong approach. I learned to be patient. After a few days, the returning warrior would always come back to his senses and become George again.

My own opportunities for adventure were not quite as exciting. As an MP officer at Fort Bragg, I kept volunteering to go up with the helicopters that managed traffic on and around the huge base. We would guide convoys toward the best route, monitor traffic congestion, and report accidents. One of the pilots finally told me I should go to flight school, I had more stick time than a lot of actual pilots. There was an increasing demand for Army pilots, but only nine women were admitted to the training every year. One problem for female applicants was that a lot of the aviation slots had combat applications. In any case, women were considered unreliable. We'll put a million dollars into her training, the program administrators would reason, then she'll decide she wants to be a mother, she'll get pregnant, and we lose a valuable asset.

I applied anyway, and was turned down. The supervisors told me that my eye test showed a probable progressive weakness in one eye. I saw pilots who wore glasses, but they had qualified before their vision deteriorated. I was terribly disappointed, but I nonetheless registered for a program offered by Embry-Riddle Aeronautical University in Daytona Beach, Florida, and earned my master's degree in aviation management. Years later, when an Army surgeon and helicopter pilot named Rhonda Cornum was shot down on a rescue mission during the first Gulf war (she was not actually piloting that flight), and was badly injured, captured by the Iraqis, and molested before she was set free, I respected her accomplishments and envied her achievement: She was a pilot.

As women stretched the Army's envelope, Rhonda Cornum was only one of the women in transportation, communications, and other fields who were authorized to venture into harm's way. In 1991 Operation Desert Storm showed everybody how quickly women in combat support roles could find themselves in the middle of battle. In that conflict, our troops slashed through Kuwait and southern Iraq so quickly—the ground war lasted only 100 hours—that they sometimes blurred the lines of combat as well as the distinction between "front" and "rear" areas. It was a smashing military triumph, but some of the 26,000 Army women deployed to the Persian Gulf ended up in the line of fire. Five Army women were killed in action, twenty-one were wounded, and two were taken prisoner by the Iraqis. Afterward, the official Pentagon evaluation concluded that women performed "admirably and without substantial friction or special considerations." The Army went back and forth for a couple of years: Was it time to open up combat specialties to women? The answer was no. Nevertheless, out of necessity in our all-volunteer Army, women were moving up the ranks and being selected for the command of units that very likely would be ordered to the middle areas of combat—not at the front, but not altogether in the rear, either. And another war was on the way.

FORT BRAGG:
HEADQUARTERS OF MACHISMO

I ALWAYS ASSUMED THAT SOME-
day I would command soldiers where bullets were flying, and I always asked myself the questions that had haunted me in basic
training: Could I do it? Could I lead soldiers into harm's way? I tried
to identify the leadership qualities I offered. In war or peace, I would
have to find the right internal balance between toughness and com-
passion—and between the feminine qualities I wanted to preserve
and the masculine culture of the Army.

Fort Bragg gave me plenty of lessons on masculinity. It was
home not only to the 82nd Airborne Division, but to the 18th Airborne Corps and the Special Operations Command. At Fort Bragg
you could feel the pulse of world affairs. Soldiers of the 82nd and the
Special Forces were the hardest-working in the Army. Like George,
they were always training to fly off to one of the world's trouble
spots at a moment's notice. And those planes took off regularly, heading for the Dominican Republic or Grenada, Kosovo, Afghanistan, or
Saudi Arabia. Fort Bragg was also a seedbed for generals. Young officers out of the Academy would fight for assignments to the 82nd,
take a staff job in the corps, go back to the 82nd to command a com-

pany, then back to the corps, rising higher every time. An ambitious officer could spend ten years climbing the ladder at Fort Bragg. Enlisted soldiers could spend a whole career there, eventually retiring as senior NCOs.

As a fledgling platoon leader, I quickly found out what I was getting into. My first company commander, a Notre Dame graduate, brought up the subject of his wife at our initial meeting. He had met her during his own first assignment, in Korea, and said he appreciated the philosophy of Asian women—subservience, taking care of their men, not speaking unless spoken to. Imagine that exchange with a new commander. It wasn't a come-on; it was a putdown on practically my first day on the job. I tried to ease out of the situation. I told him he was lucky to have found a wife on his first assignment. But he took that as a backhanded compliment and raised his eyebrows at me. Later, when our leaders were putting together contingency plans for riot control in Panama, this company commander volunteered his units for the assignment—but left out my platoon. He changed his mind when my platoon sergeant, a tough Vietnam vet who was near retirement, told him, "That's not right, sir. It's a platoon, and it shouldn't make any difference who the platoon leader is." In the end, U.S. troops were not required.

It wasn't taking me long to develop a bad feeling about my new job. On my first visit to battalion headquarters, I mentioned to the executive officer that my company commander and I might not be a great match. The XO, who was about eighty pounds overweight and looked like Old King Cole, shrugged and conceded, "He's not our strongest commander, but he's coming along."

Then when I told him about the guy's putdown, the XO said, "Well, you can work through it. Give him time. It's probably not a good mix, but then again maybe it would be the same in any of our companies."

In retrospect, he was right: That first incident was nothing compared to what was to come. My misgivings increased when my platoon sergeant, who was married, was found to be having an affair with a woman in our company; at least she was not in our platoon. He was not punished in any way. At about this time, I went to an orientation briefing for thirty-five or so newly assigned officers in units attached to the 18th Airborne Corps, but it was canceled after the video equipment broke down. As I filed out, I saw a one-star general officer standing at the door. Ever the second lieutenant who knew her place, I tried to plaster myself against a wall to let him by, but he stopped me. "Karpinski," he said, reading my name tag.

"Yes, sir," I said.

He asked where I was assigned, then invited me back for the briefing in a couple of days, after the equipment was fixed. "This is important stuff," he said.

When I went back, he and I were the only ones in the auditorium. After the lights went down and the presentation started, his hand predictably found its way to my leg. I managed to get out of that one by shifting over a seat. I was getting the impression that Fort Bragg was one challenging place for a female officer to be assigned. As a young woman, how could I gain credibility when my first problems were not with my soldiers, but with superior officers who were insulting me, dismissing me as a lightweight, and making plays for me?

When I had a chance to move on to a staff job as an intelligence officer at the corps support command, I said good riddance to my platoon. The soldiers in the ranks had performed excellently, but I couldn't say the same thing about my colleagues and superiors. At my new assignment, the colonel in charge claimed to be the kind of guy who would not cut corners for women. Men and women alike had to participate in his morning PT exercise, running in formation, and I took pride in always finishing—sometimes as a formation of one. The colonel seemed to be fairly well behaved; he would occasionally start an off-color or inappropriate joke, then stop, saying he had forgotten that Karpinski was around.

I was working in the office late one afternoon, preparing a report, when the colonel walked in and said, "Hey, Janis." He had never called me that before; I was a first lieutenant by that time. He asked for my boss, who had stepped out. Then he walked up behind me as if to see what I was working on, slipped his hand down my shirt, and fondled my breast. I bolted out of my gunmetal gray chair, whirled around, and confronted him face to face. "Well, *that's* about the dumbest thing you could do," I sputtered, and he backed off.

The next day my own boss, a major, asked me if everything was okay. I was trying to keep quiet about the incident, but the aftershocks of my latest problem with men must have shown on my face. George was in the field at the time, and I had not been able to talk to him about it. Yes, everything's fine, I said. But my new job, clearly, was an even worse fit than my old job. A few days later I was having lunch with a friend at the officers' club and told her I was looking around for yet another new assignment.

"Why?" she said in surprise. "I thought you liked the people you were working with."

I said I did (only a half-lie), but I was looking for a jump slot (a half-truth). She told me I should speak to Major Melvin C. Riley, the intelligence officer for the Seventh Special Forces Group. Special Forces, I thought to myself sarcastically: Oh sure, that'll be a real refuge from male chauvinist pigs.

As it turned out, it was. I liked Riley immediately. He had served in the Navy, got out, bought an old junker of a car with a friend, and they had driven across the country until they ran out of money. Then he had joined the Army. Such a normal guy! I told him I was looking for a new job, something where I could use my parachute training. "Any reason other than that?" he asked me.

I don't know how these people could see I had a problem, but I obviously was communicating something. No, I said again. But he kept on prodding me gently, until I conceded that a senior officer had maybe taken some liberties he shouldn't have.

"Does it involve sex?" Riley asked.

"No," I said, "but it involves fondling."

That's all he had to hear. He called the IG office—headquarters of the inspector general, the officer who investigates sensitive matters like sexual misbehavior. It took two meetings with the IG before I finally told him what had happened. "I'm concerned about whether this was really what I thought it was," I said.

"Surely, lieutenant," he responded, "you didn't take your breast and stick it in his hand. So yeah, it's what you thought it was, and it was inappropriate—unless you asked him to come over and rub your neck."

"No, sir, I certainly did not," I said.

Not too much later, the colonel with the wandering hand was relieved from command. He had been on his way to a generalship and command of the quartermaster corps. But now he was fired and left in limbo—"assigned duties," as they say—until retirement. From my perspective justice had prevailed, though I credited the system less than I did the strong advocates I had been lucky enough to find.

Major Riley gave me a job as his assistant intelligence officer and a fresh start in my career, proving that there are men in the U.S. Army who really do care about standards of professionalism.

I continued to have occasional problems with men, of course. Truth be told, I also had challenges with some of the women in my platoon. I don't know why, but female soldiers were far more reluctant to participate in our military life than the men were. Five of the thirty or so soldiers in my first MP platoon were women. Three of them were pregnant or trying to get pregnant. They were married and naturally enough wanted to have kids. But getting pregnant was also a good way to get out of PT and road duty. And you could wear civilian clothes to work, since the Army did not have a regulation pregnancy uniform. The pregnant soldiers could dress up a little and take desk jobs on the day shift, all in all a pretty good life.

Some women played into the stereotypes. A lieutenant in our sister MP company, a good officer with a college degree, went on to have a very successful military career. But she had a slightly absent-minded way about her, and the soldiers derided her constantly as a ditsy southern girl. You just didn't slide into any gray areas if you were a woman. If you had come through Fort McClellan, as this lieutenant had, you were rumored to be a lesbian. When she walked into the officers' club with a female friend, the men would whisper, That's who she's going home with tonight. If you weren't a lesbian, then you must be sleeping with every man in sight. She didn't fit into either category, and neither did I, but that didn't stop all the supposedly harmless speculation when men got together at officer's calls, professional development meetings, or a hail-and-farewell. The Army might be opening doors to women, but the old boys' network continued to have its fun at women's expense.

You just had to keep your balance through all of this. I had to be tough and aggressive to be an effective officer, but I had to temper that with my own style, and in my case that was the style of a woman. I would rather be criticized for being too soft than for being too hard. The first sergeant in one of my later commands—a hard-nosed guy who had transferred to the MPs from the infantry—pulled me aside the first time I had to call in a soldier for an Article 15, a local disciplinary procedure for minor offenses. He said, "Ma'am, you're going to do this your way, but I just want to give you some advice. Always leave them laughing. You never want to send anybody away desperate or depressed or fearful that they're in a corner and there's no way out." That advice has served me well in my career. You can discipline a soldier—even at Abu Ghraib—while letting the soldier know he or she can still earn a second chance.

Usually you have to be both good cop and bad cop. When a young sergeant in my platoon had a baby, I put her on the night shift so she could spend the day with her child. But when we suffered from a shortage of personnel, I called her in and told her she would have to go back on days. She broke into tears. "You're making me choose between my career and my child," she cried.

"No, I'm not," I told her. She herself had made the choice to take both tracks. I had one priority: our mission.

Some female soldiers over-compensated on the tough side: They became more masculine than the men. So many women wore their hair in buzz cuts that the Army put out a new regulation (ignored in Iraq) that a woman's hair could not be cut "so short as to give a masculine appearance." Army men were not allowed to wear ear studs, and some Army women refused to wear studs or earrings too—or any hint of makeup.

In Iraq, this desexualization went much further. As many as 20 percent of the soldiers who served under me in the battle zone were women, and the issue of their identity in that violent place was very real. They commonly shaved their heads for very sensible reasons. For one thing, keeping their hair clean was impossible. For another, they didn't want it tumbling out from under their Kevlar helmets in an ambush. But that didn't mean they liked the masculine style. Look at me, ma'am, some would cry. Look what I've become.

Some of the women serving in the battle zone stopped having their periods. The brigade doctors told me tension could do that. More commonly, their periods would become sporadic—and of course the spotting always seemed to begin while a woman was on guard duty or patrol. Some women would take birth-control pills just so they could have a regular cycle. Even then, keeping clean in those austere conditions was a mighty task when some of the latrines were so filthy you couldn't get within six feet of them. I would be in favor of a pill that turned off your menstrual cycle completely during the time you were in a battle zone. If such pills were offered, I know that a lot of military women would take them.

A bulky combat uniform really completed the masculine look in the field. While I was inspecting a reconstruction project at one prison in Iraq, the shift supervisor gave me an excellent two-hour tour and progress briefing. As we were leaving, my security guy commented, "He's a really good NCO, isn't he?"

"He who?" I asked.

"The NCO in charge, the one who just gave you a tour," he said.

I couldn't believe it. I turned to my sergeant major and asked him if he recalled the NCO's name.

"I think his name was Sergeant Jacobs," he said unhelpfully.

"Not his, it's her. He's a she," said my security man.

"He is not a she, he's a he," insisted the sergeant major.

He announced that he was going to go back and talk to her again to settle the issue. He returned chastened, shaking his head. "Ma'am, she is definitely a woman," he said.

On the flip side, Army women who actually tried to look like women sometimes went too far. Although they were supposed to wear their hair longer than a man's, women were forbidden to style it extravagantly or to put on heavy makeup or wear colorful finger-nail polish. But women were always pushing the limits, especially during stateside duty. The pregnant women, in particular, took full advantage of their permission to wear "appropriate" civilian clothes. They would apply a touch of nail polish, then a darker color, then a wild design until somebody stopped them. Their hairstyles would gradually get wilder until hair was popping up all over the place. They must have been traveling to their offices without the required hat, unless these hairstyles were spring-loaded.

Women had one fashion arena all to themselves: They could express themselves through their underwear. Female soldiers had the widest variety and most unique collection of undergarments you could imagine. These were the only elements of clothing the Army did not regulate, so women took full advantage. You would see clotheslines hung with leopard-print panties, fur bras (something I had never seen before), and every design imaginable—stripes, pais-ley, polka dots, neon colors, frills, and lace. Sometimes an Army barracks looked like Sunday morning after a busy night at the whorehouse.

The Army's regulations did have some purpose other than to de-feminize us, as I discovered. Before one formal function at Fort Bragg, I bent the rules by keeping my fingernails long after having a manicure. Two days later, I had a jump. The wind was a bit high on the ground, a condition that can cause your parachute to reinflate and start to drag you. So when I hit the ground, I executed a PLF (parachute landing fall) and reached up to pull the Capewell canopy release, which collapses the parachute. As I grabbed for the release, the parachute risers, the lines attaching the harness to the canopy, snagged one of my long fingernails and broke it across the middle. The wound bled profusely, but I was relieved that I still had a finger.

After that, I cut my nails off and left them off. I gave other women in the field the same advice. Sometimes I would hear: It's okay, I'll put gloves on. But gloves or no gloves, nails that extend beyond the length of your finger are a hazard.

Over the years, I became comfortable with the duality of being a woman and an Army officer. When I had my official photo taken for the board that was considering me for a generalship, I made sure I was Army regulation all the way: hair pulled tight, minimal makeup, modest earrings—on second thought, no earrings at all. Once again, it was a matter of balance. I had to look feminine, but not too feminine. I'm still maintaining that balance. After going through a gauntlet of gropes, wolf whistles, invitations to bed, and other travails of a blonde woman in the Army, now I'm described on some unfriendly websites as looking more masculine than Janet Reno. The real me is somewhere between those two extremes.

Choosing a military life did require sacrifices. My husband and I decided we would not have children. As career Army people, we were always on the move and often flying off to different assignments. Even when we were based together, as a Special Forces officer George spent most of his life in the field. If we had kids, I knew I would have to take most of the responsibility for raising them. But I could not do that and also meet the responsibilities of a full-time officer in the Army. I also needed George's calmer temperament to make me a better person; his parenting skills would have exceeded mine. While I was always happiest jumping out of airplanes, he was always happiest when he was serving, be it our country or our families. But I couldn't ask him to become a househusband. If you're going to be competitive as a combat arms officer, you have to take the jobs that are most demanding, the ones that put you out there in the field.

I also was not sure I wanted my kids raised in the Army lifestyle. Army families are more fragmented, scattered, and rootless than the happy homestead of my own memories. I am amazed by those female soldiers who can maintain a career and a stable home while showing their kids the world. But when I think of an Army family I recall the one I encountered during a stateside assignment. The father, a lieutenant colonel provost marshal in his forties, was overweight and out of shape. He invited us to his house once to welcome new officers to our command group. As we arrived, we heard him and his wife arguing loudly inside. He then gave us a tour of all the problems with the place that he had to fix. His son was sitting in his room above the garage, eating Cheese Nips and peanut butter, about fifty pounds overweight. When his father and the guests walked in, the kid just sat there in the middle of all that junk food, watching television and being as rude as he could possibly be. Later the lieutenant colonel, who doubled as a minister, was drumming up business, offering to marry the new officer and his girlfriend. Then our host turned to me and said, "Janis, you should consider having children soon. Put your Army career aside." And I was thinking: yeah, right, for a great life like this.

I could not put my Army career aside, even for a family, but I also had to recognize the limits of that career. After I had been at Fort Bragg for a few years, it suddenly occurred to me—and this was no flash of brilliance—that because women could not serve in combat, no woman would ever be chosen as the Army chief of staff, or would ever be chairman of the joint chiefs, or would ever be secretary of the Army. Those jobs did and should go to officers with combat experience. Perhaps women will get there some day. When I was at Fort Bragg, only about 2 percent of an elite group like the 82nd Airborne was made up of women in peripheral roles. Today it's up to 3 percent, about 420 women. The first GI Jane doll (companion to GI Joe) had an 82nd Airborne patch on her shoulder.

How far could I take my leadership potential? In Iraq, when our resources were stretched to the breaking point, I would remind my soldiers of the story of British Field Marshal William Slim. Assigned to root out the Japanese from Burma toward the end of World War II but gravely lacking in air transport and other logistical support, Slim cobbled together his climactic offensive using teak rafts, building roads and airfields as he advanced. Lesson: You must, and you can, make do with what you have.

In another way, I was just as impressed by the case of Admiral Jeremy Boorda. He had risen to Chief of Naval Operations (CNO), the Navy's top job, as a "sailor's sailor," the first CNO to have come up from the enlisted ranks. He had lacked the usual qualifications for officers aiming at the very top—a degree from the Naval Academy and service in one of the elite branches, such as the aviators or submariners. With that background, he once said he always felt he was missing the credentials that would give him automatic status in the Navy. He always had to prove himself to his colleagues. I understand that pressure—and the vital necessity of keeping your feet and keeping your balance under its weight. Boorda faltered. In 1996, after *Newsweek* questioned whether he was authorized to wear a certain decoration, he went home for lunch and shot himself to death.

I kept plowing ahead, taking every challenge they would give me. At Fort Bragg I campaigned to go to jump-master school and was admitted. To pass, I had to prove that I could jump in any conceivable condition—at night, in high winds, landing in trees. During my career I have jumped into snow, water, fields of flowers, and mud. You drill, drill, and drill again until you can respond automatically to any adversity. The jump master also must check the equipment on other jumpers before they take the plunge. It's an enormous responsibility. You're the one who puts them out of the airplane. The first command is, "Stand in the door!" You stand there only for an instant. You can see the whole world before you, but not what is going to happen to you out in those crosscurrents. And you never look down.

JANIS OF ARABIA

I HAD JOINED THE ARMY TO GET
what the recruiting posters offered, adventure and travel. I wanted
to do what soldiers do—like jump out of airplanes—and in the back
of my mind was that shimmering, schoolgirl vision of the pyramids.

That vision grew more substantial when my husband was assigned to Arabic language school while we were stationed at Fort
Bragg. As I studied informally along with George, helping him
practice and memorize his flash cards, I began to pick up the rudi-
ments of the language myself. We had a common friend, Steve
Beitler, another Special Forces officer, who was desperately trying
to finagle an assignment to Saudi Arabia—no easy task, since he
was Jewish and had an Israeli visa in his passport, both red flags to
the Saudis. At the same time, the headlines were dominated by Is-
rael's 1982 invasion of Lebanon. We all spent hours talking about
Mideast politics and history, to the point where the subject became
a passion. I imagined Beirut as Steve described it, the Paris of the
Middle East, with its outdoor cafés, rich coffee, and cosmopolitan
life, now torn apart by war. Steve was eager for any opportunity to
visit the region. He wanted to marry his fiancée, Debby, and take

her to Saudi Arabia. He succeeded in each undertaking. He married his sweetheart in an elegant wedding in Chicago, and they went to Saudi Arabia for their honeymoon. Steve remained in Saudi Arabia to complete his tour, while Debby returned home to Chicago.

I wanted to do more than visit. Why couldn't I get an assignment to the Middle East as well? Steve told me to forget that idea. The Army would never send me to a place where I would have to wear a veil and where our allies would refuse to deal with me because I was a woman. I didn't argue with him, but I refused to accept what he said. Women in the Middle East *couldn't* be treated as badly as the books claimed they were. And I was becoming as obsessed with Arabian dreams as Steve and George were. I went to the advanced MP course at Fort McClellan later in 1982, and there we had major blocks of instruction on antiterrorism and counterterrorism. When we talked about the Middle East, I already knew a lot about the issues there and even spoke some of the language.

Our discussions echoed in my mind many years later. The Middle East is so torn by so many centuries of conflict, we agreed, that the United States must never commit its forces there without a clear and attainable exit strategy. But now we have done just that. Before marching into Iraq, we didn't even have a strategy for sustaining our military advances. I guess the war planners thought that as we liberated the Iraqis they would immediately and independently form a U.S.-style democracy. The Iraqis certainly wanted to be freed from the tyranny of Saddam, but they had never known freedom or even free thinking. They looked to us for direction. When they saw looters take to the streets unhindered by U.S. troops, many Iraqis joined in, assuming that looting was part of the new freedom we had given them. We could have shown them a better way, but we failed to do so.

After advanced training, I got my first coveted overseas assignment as operations officer on an antiterrorism task force based in Mannheim, West Germany. The Red Army Faction and other German terror groups were still active. The MP mission was to guard military facilities, including nuclear sites, and to serve as an immediate response force after any terrorist actions. My boss was a great guy named Marion who preferred his middle name, Tom. He was one of those Army officers who worked easily with a woman. ("I think women do better work on terrorism," he told me once. "I know my first wife really terrorized me.")

In West Germany I joined George, who already was working in Mannheim as operations officer in an infantry battalion. This was our dream—traveling the world together in the Army's married-couples program. Of course, the Army had the last laugh. In the first year of our "joint" posting, George was on the road 294 days for infantry exercises. In the second year, we stopped counting. I could take it. George always expected me to be able to find my way. I tried never to let him down.

I took my own opportunities to hit the road. I moved to a new job, also in Mannheim, that involved traveling throughout Europe—Turkey, Greece, Italy, Spain—inspecting U.S.-bound shipments for customs violations. The problem had grown out of a Vietnam-era policy to expedite shipments for senders and receivers who were established partners. The idea worked too well. These so-called "closed loops" proved to be ideal for shipping drugs, weapons, and other contraband into the United States. Our job was to make sure that the foreign shippers were involved in legitimate business transactions and to randomly inspect some of the shipments. To me, the travel was more interesting than the work, especially when we were assigned to launch a new round of investigations—in the Middle East.

This was my chance to measure all I had learned, all the topics of our spirited debates, against reality. I hoped the region would meet my expectations and be every bit as exotic as I had imagined. Our first stop was rather anticlimactic. In Bahrain, the Arab women did indeed seem to be better off than the books had indicated. Our flight was staffed by beautiful, Bahrain-based attendants dressed in modern uniforms. They were said to be the girlfriends of rich Saudis. Other Bahraini women went about their business with or without veils, as they chose. You would see them in restaurants and driving their own cars. When we took the short hop to Dhahran, Saudi Arabia, I expected more of the same. We got off the plane, I looked around, then looked again. The first question that popped into my mind on Saudi soil was: Are there any women anywhere in this country?

Women seemed to have disappeared from the face of the earth. Men piloted and docked the plane. Men escorted us to immigration and through customs. A male driver from the embassy met us—and handed me what looked like a bulky, black bathrobe to put on. This was my first encounter with an *abaya*, the cloak that covers Arab women from neck to toe. After putting it on, I was given a *shayla*, the black head covering. I managed to avoid wearing a *burqa*, the face covering that is often fashioned from a mesh of copper or some other impenetrable metal. In full regalia, Saudi women essentially disappear; they are like black ghosts floating in the background, tethered to the men who dominate their existence (at least in public). Even as a woman, I had no access to the women of Saudi Arabia, even casually. Once I said to the driver, "If you just stop, could I say hello to one of them?"

"No," he said immediately. "Please don't. It would be a problem."

So I backed off. The Saudis clearly did not want any foreign ideas penetrating those veils. I realized that what I'd read about the subservient status of Arab women was accurate to the extreme in Saudi Arabia, if not understated.

In Dhahran, we went to a restaurant for dinner. That was no casual operation with me, a woman, along. The American NCO said, "Ma'am, you're going to have to cover your head." And when we got to the restaurant, he warned that "they probably won't want you to sit at the same table." Another officer had brought along his wife so that I wouldn't have to sit alone, facing the wall. In the end, since we were Americans and I was properly covered from head to toe, the management let us sit together. At other times, I did see Saudi women in restaurants, on special occasions, seated in special family sections. A hand, often wearing a glove, would emerge from the silent black ghost, take a piece of food, and draw it under the veil. What a pleasant way to enjoy a night out with your husband!

At least the food lived up to my dreams of exotic Arabia. I cannot think of those lands today without remembering the scents of cardamom, saffron, and garlic. From its history as a crossroads on the trade routes linking India, the Middle East, and Africa, Saudi Arabia has borrowed the clarified butter, curries, and flat breads of India, the pickles and yogurts of Iran, stuffed grape leaves from the Mediterranean, mint tea from Morocco, and other dishes from the far corners of the ancient world. I learned to avoid camel meat (greasy) and the great delicacies presented at a banquet: the eyeballs of a sheep, goat, or lamb as well as the brain, served in a head pulled apart by the jaw. I did try a piece of brain by accident once, thinking it was fish; it tasted like a boiled, dirty woolen sock. I prefer to remember the tables piled with roast meats, often stuffed with hard-boiled eggs, accompanied by saffron rice, soups, juices, and wonderful fruits.

The traditional riches of Saudi Arabia were more fascinating than the oil wealth. The spice markets overwhelmed your senses.

The big, burlap spice bags were arranged by degrees of pungency, so that a shopper could proceed from the mildest cardamom to the hottest peppers, sampling tastes and smells. The merchants offered magnificently plump olives and dried lemons that you would crush in your hand and sprinkle into hot tea. Other markets specialized in gold. In Riyadh's gold market one night, I watched a dozen black-clad women, escorted by a couple of men from their family, picking through the glittering wares, probably seeking to stock a wedding dowry. They chose from among dinner-plate-size discs of gold and displays of sumptuous jewelry. When I remarked on a dazzling collection of necklaces, I was corrected: Those were not necklaces; they were golden belts.

I got the point of all this in later years, as I attended numerous weddings in the Arab world. The point was that your daughter had to have a more extravagant wedding than any that had ever gone before. Families seemed to live for weddings. Preparations would start a week beforehand, when a bride-to-be would have her body waxed, removing every last extraneous hair. Delicate henna designs would be applied to her hands and feet. Her hair would be perfectly styled, and on the big day she would be doused in what seemed like three gallons of perfume. Then she was ready for The Dress. At one of the more lavish weddings I attended, the bride—daughter of a pearl merchant who also had made millions in oil—emerged in a white gown and train encrusted with pearls and diamonds. She stepped onto a path of freshly strewn flower petals. When the overhead lights focused on her, she lit up like a roman candle of sparkling jewelry. She labored up two steps to the runway of the wedding hall, so weighed down by her riches that she could hardly walk.

The 500 women guests in the room (the men partied separately) were only less dazzling by comparison with the bride. They wore elegant formal wear copied from originals by the likes of Christian

Dior and Nicole Miller. As women who could be seen only by other women, the younger among them chose creations with plunging backs, daring necklines, and slits up to the hip. There had to be $4 million worth of jewelry in the room before the bride even made her appearance. Part of the show was intended for attending mothers, who would size up likely prospects for their single sons. From my perspective, it was simply the gaudiest fashion show I had ever seen—until word spread that the groom and his attendants were arriving. Like a wave, the black cloaks came out and spread across the hall, covering every bejeweled hairdo and impressive cleavage in sight. The bride alone remained uncloaked and dazzling, exempt because only her future husband and other men from her close family would behold her.

Within hours—especially if she was a Saudi woman—a bride would have to return to the sorority of black ghosts. As the guardian of Mecca, Saudi Arabia considered itself the exemplar of Koranic traditions, and one of those traditions held that an uncovered woman who excited a man was to blame for anything that might happen to her as a result. During the first Gulf war, three American female soldiers, properly uniformed, found themselves sharing an elevator with two Saudi privates at a military installation in Riyadh that the Saudis shared with us. Between floors, one of the Saudis suddenly grabbed an American and started to kiss her. She quickly kicked him in the groin and pushed him away. The Saudis then began screaming and demanding (in vain) that the women be arrested for humiliating them.

Had the women in the elevator been Saudis, the incident would have been no laughing matter. The country's *muttawa*, or religious police, were everywhere. They wore untrimmed beards, a sign of their religiosity, and would stalk through public places in their sandals, carrying canes and peering from side to side like Grinches on patrol. If they saw minor offenses, they would whack the offender on the back of the legs. If a woman raised her *abaya* to try on shoes in a store, she risked six whacks. If a man was seen chatting with a woman in public, she got her whacks, and he would have to run fast to avoid a solid blow to the head. I made sure to keep well covered at all times in public. I slipped only once. I had stopped by a women's shop in a little mall to purchase a few items of civilian clothing. As I was paying the Filipino woman behind the register, she gestured toward the door. There stood a *muttawa*, staring at me. I realized that although I was wearing an *abaya*, I had left the front open, exposing my shirt and jeans. I quickly pulled it closed. The *muttawa* nodded in approval and continued on his way.

God help those charged with serious religious violations. A woman caught having an affair can be in grave danger: Your own relatives can decide that the family's humiliation is so great that you must die. Executions for any variety of infractions would be scheduled for town squares on Friday. Depending on the crime, the condemned prisoners could be stoned to death or lose their heads. One executioner, in an interview with a newspaper, explained that he kept his sword as sharp as possible so that he could cut off heads and hands cleanly and humanely, as the Koran demanded.

That sense of rigid, brutal propriety was everywhere as we flew in our C-12 aircraft from Dhahran to Riyadh to Jeddah, crossing huge swaths of empty desert. Riyadh, the capital, tried to help its citizens forget that they lived in the center rack of an oven by putting up elaborate fountains throughout the city, spraying water and maybe a touch of humidity into the air. Jeddah, the port city on the Red Sea, passed for a liberal enclave in Saudi Arabia: Every once in a while you would encounter a woman without a face covering. The city had huge, empty parking lots, well lighted and stretching almost to the horizon—all of them full of vehicles, I was told, when pilgrims converged on Mecca for the Hajj, the annual display of Islam's immense reach and power.

We arrived in Egypt after a week or so in Saudi Arabia. I felt as if I had been relieved of an oppressive weight. A few black ghosts drifted through the streets, but other women wore colorful robes or Western dress. As a secular republic with something of a superiority complex, Egypt is regarded by Saudis as *haram*—a shameful place. I looked up an Egyptian officer, Abdullah Latif al Rizk, who had attended the advanced MP class with me in Fort McClellan and had become my friend, helping me with my Arabic. In our classroom debates, he had argued (much as the Saudis had) that Americans must be involved but discreet in our commitment to the region, generous in our military support while allowing the host country to appear self-sufficient. But in Cairo, Latif didn't make me invisible at all. He took me home to meet his mother and sisters, and I peppered them with questions that had preoccupied me in Saudi Arabia. What is it like under those metal face plates? I asked his mother. Don't you suffocate?

She just laughed. "Yes, it's very hot, but this is the custom," she said. "This is the life. If your husband tells you to do this, you do it." No longer, Latif emphasized. All his sisters had gone to college, wore Western clothes, and worked. No veils for them.

We had a wonderful time in Cairo, with its chaotic traffic, its filth and beggars—and its aura of freedom after Saudi Arabia. My decision to join the Army was confirmed when I drove outside of town and gazed upon the actual pyramids. It is hard to convey the sense of satisfaction and connection I felt as the wonder from my schoolgirl days came back to me and I stood before the monuments themselves. How could an ancient civilization have imagined these works, and designed and engineered them so indestructibly in the middle of nowhere? And actually marshaled the labor to build them with so few of the tools we have today? The arrogance, ambition, and brutality that these elegant structures represented! I must have walked around the Sphinx a hundred times. None of the tourist caravans, the light shows, or the camel rides offered at its feet could dent its pride.

When I got back to Germany, I read everything I could find about the Middle East and stepped up my language lessons. I desperately wanted to get back to the region, especially to Saudi Arabia. I had to get behind those walls and under those veils to discover more about the lives of Saudi women. I felt that I had gotten close in Jeddah, toward the end of my stay. I had strolled into a perfume shop to sample one of the most fragrant and expensive perfumes in the world, *dehn al-oud*, extracted from the *oud* tree of India. I was delighted to see that the saleswoman was dressed entirely in black in the Saudi style, not in the haphazard way of the foreigners who usually work in shops. "I'm surprised you're here," I said in Arabic. "It's so good to meet a Saudi woman."

She responded in perfect English: "I'm not Saudi," she said. "I'm from Bahrain, but I married a Saudi."

I had to keep trying. Life under the sway of the *muttawa* was so strict, and women's public personas so limited—could it be like that in their homes, as well? Was there no respite from the all-encompassing power of a religion that could summon people from across the world to Mecca, that could shut down a capital city five times a day for prayer call? Or was the religion itself a greater respite from life's burdens than I could understand? I had to study more. I had to read the Koran. I had to find out more from my side of the wall, and in time I would.

THE WEEKEND WARRIOR

BY THE TIME I RETURNED FROM
my antiterrorism task force assignment, my life and career had split
into two strands. As always, I was in love with soldiering, and now I
was equally obsessed with the Middle East. You could have found
the seeds of these interests in the towhead from Rahway who admired photographs of her father in his Army uniform, then turned
the page of a textbook to discover those pyramids for the first time.
It is still difficult for me to believe, as I count down the days toward
my formal retirement, that when these strands actually came together, during my assignment in Iraq, disaster struck. What should
have been the culmination of my career—a major command in the
Middle East—became instead the greatest challenge of my life.

I was riding high when I came back to the States from Germany.
I was a captain in the U.S. Army about to take my first real command,
in charge of a 180-soldier MP company at Fort McPherson, Georgia.
My husband took a job in nearby Fort Gillem, where he served as the
operations officer for a recruiting brigade. Once again, we had demanding jobs that required us to give the Army much more than routine, 9-to-5 days. We were beginning to get the idea that for all the

Army's togetherness programs, we were bound to spend an inordinate amount of time apart from each other. But whenever our marriage appeared to be slipping into a hello/good-bye relationship, we would find an island of time to ourselves in the sea of Army responsibilities. Yes, we had to break a lot of plans, postpone a lot of vacations, but we managed.

As I prepared to lead my new company, I encountered a familiar obstacle in the MP corps—its men. The battalion I joined had never had a ranking female officer before. That created perplexity in some minds. The base honor guard, a military organization's epitome of rigid backbones and spit and polish, was drawn from the MP corps. How could the honor guard preserve its aura if it was led by someone wearing a skirt? The battalion commander, an infantry guy who believed he was far more capable than he was, told me I could command the MP company but would not be permitted to serve as commander of troops for formal ceremonies.

Hold on a second, I responded. That's an important part of the job. Fort McPherson, located in Atlanta, served as headquarters for the Forces Command (FORSCOM) and the Third Army, and the Second Army was based not far away at Fort Gillem. That meant the base was crawling with generals, whose historic brick homes stretched in a "generals' row" along the parade field, and there were many calls for the honor guard. In fact, an important change-of-command ceremony was already on our schedule.

The way that happened was pure serendipity. In the early-morning fog one day, I had had my troops out practicing our skills. As we marched and handled weapons, this guy in gray shorts and a PT shirt reading "Army" came running by. He stopped when he saw us, grabbed a weapon from a soldier, and said, "Do you know how to do this? Where's the NCO?" he demanded. "Give me some commands."

We had no idea who he was, but the NCO started shouting out commands: Right shoulder, arms! Left shoulder, arms! The guy went through the manual of arms, tossed the rifle back, and told the troops, "You look pretty sharp." Then he turned to me and said, "Who are you?"

I extended my hand to introduce myself, and told him I was Captain Karpinski, the company commander. He said, "Well, I'm General Palastra. I'm coming in as the new FORSCOM Commander." Call me emotional, but I almost fainted. A few days later, we were scheduled to conduct the ceremony when he assumed his command.

Now the only question was whether I would preside over the occasion. My battalion commander simply did not want a woman serving as commander of troops. But he focused on another issue: trousers. A woman's dress uniform called for a skirt and did not include trousers. So I bought a pair of men's formal trousers and had them tailored to my female shape. When I got the uniform back from the tailor, I was ordered to model it for three men—a lieutenant colonel, a major, and the command sergeant major—sitting on chairs and observing me as if I were a piece of meat on a hook. "Turn forty-five degrees," they would tell me. Then, "Turn forty-five degrees" again. The lieutenant colonel, my battalion commander, suggested putting a padded belt around my waist to make my appearance more masculine, or at least less feminine.

That's where I stopped the show. Careful to preserve my military bearing (a female officer can never appear to be "emotional"), I pointed out, "I am a woman. You are not going to disguise me."

"I don't believe anybody asked you for your opinion," my commander responded.

"Well," I said, "I'm standing here in the middle of the room in this inappropriate situation, and you're discussing me like I'm not even here, sir."

"We've never had a female on the parade field," he said.

Times are changing, I thought to myself.

I decided I had no choice but to appeal up the chain of command, something I ordinarily hate doing. In this case, I had a personal connection. I knocked on General Joseph Palastra's door, and he listened patiently to the story of my drill uniform. When I got to the part about the padded belt, the general said, "You are not serious, Captain." And I said, "Yes, sir, I am serious."

Palastra immediately picked up the phone and called my battalion commander. "You're not going to disguise her in any way," he ordered. "Next time you'll want to put a mustache on her."

General Palastra never went out of his way to support me after that, but I knew he was always there. I conducted his ceremony proudly, and he seemed to be kind of proud himself to have a woman as commander of troops.

He couldn't resolve my main frustration, of course. For every good guy I encountered in the Army, I ran into an even more irritating nemesis. My own branch, with its oversupply of sidetracked infantrymen and insecure "little guns," seemed particularly averse to the rise of women. I loved my job as company commander, but it brought with it a parade of woeful enlisted women seeking my help and advice. Some of them were still teenagers, or in their very early twenties. They had come out of training to find themselves outnumbered twenty to one by men in their first MP assignments. And according to the dictum, if they weren't gay, they had to be available. Men hit on them constantly: How about dinner? How about lunch? Why don't we go out for a drink? Don't go out with him, go out with me. Many of the women felt besieged. They couldn't take a step without the wolves closing in. All too typically, a young woman would settle on one guy as a way to deflect all the others. Three weeks later, they would get married. A year later, he would get orders or she would get orders, and it would all be over. The divorce rate was extremely high. And too many disposable marriages left children behind along with broken homes.

I would try to counsel these forlorn women before they tied the knot. You don't know this man, I would say. Why do you think you know him? You're from opposite ends of the country. And they would say, "Ma'am, you don't know what it's like being in that barracks if you're not married." I heard that repeated again and again. It was heartbreaking. A young woman would join the Army seeking an education and a career, and six months later she would be married and pregnant at nineteen.

Women who did run the gauntlet came out flintier. They had climbed the ladder to become sergeants, competing with men all the way. Some of them tried to fit in by toughening their demeanor and dirtying up their vocabulary. I advised against that approach, because fair or not, loutish behavior reflects worse on women than it does on men. After I had been in charge for five or six months, I noticed that the women in my company were starting to look more like women. I hoped they were seeing me as a role model: You could become a master jumper and maintain your femininity, too.

After nine and a half years, I found I was struggling against the traditions of this man's Army as vigorously as ever, but with a difference. The competition was beginning to wear me down. Perhaps I had joined the service too early in its evolution to become a revolutionary. Perhaps I had become a guinea pig instead. When I accepted my commission, I had told myself that I would give the Army ten years, then reassess. That time had come, and I decided to look around.

I asked my MP branch manager what the Army had in store for me next. Could I get back on jump status? No, I was told. I should expect a staff job for two or three years—not much fun at all after

the challenge of my first command. I played my Army career over
and over again in my mind. There were times, after a tough jump
or some spirited maneuvers, when I loved this job so much they
didn't have to pay me. I was climbing the ladder at a good pace and
expected a promotion to major within a few months. But at every
turn, I could be sure of running into some colonel who would want
to put a padded belt around me, or some traditional Army lady
showing off her hat and white gloves like Little Bo Peep. I remembered the exhilaration of basic training—the marching soldiers, the
monster battle tanks, the 300 sit-ups—and I realized that those moments of excitement and commitment were growing fewer and far
between.

I couldn't believe it, but civilian life was starting to look good.
Atlanta felt like a young city, full of opportunities for professional
women. I could see myself as an executive with Delta Airlines (even
if they wouldn't let me jump out of their planes). The Atlanta police
department was interested in recruiting me. So was a big private investigating company. George was working at the recruiting command in Marietta, and we had bought a house in Atlanta. We could
finally put down roots somewhere. In the end, the decision wasn't
so hard to make.

I *still* loved being a soldier. Yes, the job was wearing me down, but
I still had the uniform, the parachute pin on my pocket, the service to
the American flag, and a strong sense of identity. And I had a significant career investment. A friend of mine who had already retired
from the service told me I would be foolish not to consider joining
the Reserves or the National Guard as a way to continue building on
the military career I had begun. At first I had trouble picturing myself
in either organization. I shared the contemptuous attitude that most
active-duty soldiers show toward those units. I would not even consider the National Guard, whose troops I caricatured as a bunch of

long-haired, stubbly bearded beer-bellies. (I was wrong; in fact, some of the finest officers and soldiers I served with in Iraq were members of National Guard units.) I also had little respect for the Reserves, the "weekend warriors" who were only "pretending" to be soldiers. If I was frustrated as a woman soldier, how much more frustrated would I be as a woman Reserve soldier?

And yet. The Reserve soldiers I actually had run into during my service had seemed squared-away and professional. There was a real place for them in the Army, supporting the combat units and providing peacekeepers and nation-builders. I could settle down into a civilian job and still pursue a military career part-time. I could continue to earn military retirement points and continue to wear the uniform, and I could get those major's leaves that were coming my way. The Reserves needed officers—and women officers in particular at a time when a disproportionate number of women were choosing to join the Reserves over the regular Army. I went down to the Reserves' recruiting office. The officer on duty said there were no openings at the moment, but he put my name and qualifications into the database. The next day he called. There was a position at Dobbins Air Force Base, which was even closer to my house than McPherson. In 1987, I made the leap.

The new civilian part of my life was totally strange. I took the job with the investigating company, where I specialized in documenting fraud against rental-car companies. My boss was retired from the Army's criminal investigation command, and he was looking for someone who brought military discipline to the table. He knew that I could set and uphold standards. But although I had been buying business suits for some time, preparing for this contingency, I was not comfortable in the civilian workplace. It was unsettling to set off to work out of uniform, with my hair down, wearing makeup, jewelry, and longer fingernails. The women I encountered at work looked like fashion queens to me. They must be rising long before dawn to put themselves together like that. I quickly found myself missing the little courtesies and disciplines of military life, and the sense of mission. So many of these civilians seemed complacent, unmotivated. When I addressed one of them as "sir," he looked at me strangely; nobody would ever dream of calling me "ma'am." Few of these civilians could give a briefing, or even stand up and speak in public. I volunteered to teach in an adult literacy program and discovered that a lot of people in high places could not read, either.

I also had to get used to the new rhythms of the Army Reserve. After a decade of 24/7 duty, I now put on the uniform for only one weekend a month and two weeks in the summer. My promotion to major came through a few months after I left active duty. My Reserve unit at Dobbins, where I had served as chief of the counterintelligence branch, was deactivated, but I got another good post with the Third Army at Fort McPherson. I became a targeting officer—or "targeteer," as we were called—working up defensive and offensive contingency plans. I was assigned the countries of Yemen, Iraq, the United Arab Emirates, and Kuwait, becoming an expert on their societies in the then-unlikely event that we would be drawn into conflict in the Middle East. You can abandon a lot of your military culture when you go from being a warrior to a weekend warrior, but I didn't. I had a real-time job that required me to keep up to date on current affairs and attend intel briefs. And I still had the sense that I was fighting for the cause of women in the military. Women are lazy? No. Women are too emotional? No. Women are out of shape? No. And now I had a new cause. Reservists are inferior to active-duty soldiers? No way!

After a few months, I had an opportunity to merge my military and civilian lives. Lieutenant Colonel Jes Ramos, chief of staff at Fort McPherson, urged me to apply for a senior civilian position at the base as director of security plans and training. It was a great job, one fit for a colonel if the Army had filled it from within. When I showed up for the interview, a retired lieutenant colonel was sitting in the waiting room. He told me he was certain he would get the position, and I said, "Well, it's good to have confidence going into an interview."

Then he looked at me and asked, "Is there a secretarial position open? Is that why you're here?"

"No," I said. "I'm your competition."

I told that story to the interviewing board. It got a laugh—and maybe it helped me get the job.

When I got out of the Army, I should have realized how hard it would be to get the Army out of me. Now I was happy to find myself working at one Army job as a civilian on weekdays, then putting on my uniform for another Army job on duty weekends. I learned to appreciate my fellow reservists. They brought in a variety of qualifications and qualities from lives outside the military. They were generally more easygoing, with a better sense of humor than the cloistered, regimented officers of the regular Army.

Only one thing was wrong with my new life. In 1990 George received orders for an unaccompanied year-long tour in Yemen. As a Special Forces officer, he had spent a lot of time away from me already. But when I took him to the airport and dropped him off, I just didn't feel ready to say good-bye for so long. So I began preparing to visit him for a month halfway through his tour. Yemen was one of the countries in my military portfolio in any case, so I studied and researched before I went and took along a camera for hours of filming. The country was in the beginning stages of a strategic upheaval: A merger was in the works between the leftist People's Democratic Republic in the South and the more pro-Western Yemen Arab Republic of the North. The populace ratified the unity constitution in 1991, though civil unrest continued for several years.

At the same time, across Saudi Arabia's desert to the north, Iraq's Saddam Hussein was making preparations for his August invasion of Kuwait, the summer surprise that was about to throw our lives into turmoil. I was determined to give a brilliant country briefing on my return. And I also looked forward to another opportunity to try to peek under the veil of an Arab society.

• • •

LANDING IN YEMEN WAS LIKE ENTERING A Medieval time warp. At the airport in Sanaa, which soon was to become the capital of the reunified country, the female immigration agent beamed at my unpolished Arabic and grabbed my hand in both of hers. "Welcome, welcome," she said. "We *like* to see American women." The fact that I could enjoy the woman's smile—she had no *burqa* hiding her face—and that she had a job stamping passports heartened me. The introduction confirmed my working theory: If you're an Arab woman, the farther you get from Riyadh the better. "I like to see Yemeni women, too," I told her.

The skin-baking heat and the dusty desert air enveloped me like old friends: They told me that I was back in this exotic part of the world that I had begun to discover. Societies had risen and fallen in these terraced hills for thousands of years. Timeless cities of earthen buildings, their glassless windows rimmed by white gypsum, rose above the sands like gingerbread houses. As at the pyramids of Giza, you could reach out here and touch ancient history.

When I look back at my time in Yemen—and I write this after many more years spent living and working in the Middle East—what stands out is the essential goodness and kindness of the people I encountered at every step. Their sense of history lends a kind of cultural stability that balances the political turbulence and excesses of oil wealth. The religion that causes such consternation and even fear in the West shows its gentle side in the desert countries—again, when politics allows it to. Ramadan is a season of fasting, of recognizing how much you have and how many ways you have been blessed. It is a season also of giving, of opening your home to those in need. The tenets of Islam instruct Muslims to share what they have during the rest of the year, as well. The poor man in Yemen, with two coins in his pocket, will give one to someone poorer. People might not have much in their kitchens, but they always set a place at the table for one more. They believe that a stranger may be God or an angel in disguise.

God does not always come calling, of course. The region's nomadic history includes traditions of lawlessness and violence, as well, something Americans can recognize in the frontier mentality that is part of their own country's history. It all comes together at the rich market in Sanaa. There a camel turns an ancient wheel, grinding sesame seeds as camels have done for centuries. There gold merchants offer handcrafted Yemeni jewelry of the highest quality, and women apply perfume and the lacy designs of henna dye to their hands and feet. (How they loved seeing their handiwork against the contrast of my pale skin!) And there men shop for bazookas, handguns, AK47s, and the daggers, or *khunjars*, that every man in Yemen seems to be carrying under his robe.

Everywhere I went, the Yemenis I met seemed to want to treat Americans well—perhaps because their nation, North Yemen, was insecure about its pending reunification with the socialists of South Yemen, who had maintained a separate government for nearly a quarter of a century. I had learned how to show respect. Because I visited during Ramadan, I wore long-sleeved blouses and ankle-length skirts or trousers, and I covered my head. The women around me, unlike the black ghosts in Saudi Arabia, reflected Yemen's links across the Red Sea to Africa. All but the most conservative wore colorful *abayas* in oranges, yellows, and reds, often patterned in contrast to the equally bright, solid colors of their *shaylas*. They did not look to be as reticent as the women of Saudi Arabia, and they were not. As some of them prepared for an *iftar*, the meal breaking the daylong fast of Ramadan, they suggested that a friend in the U.S. Embassy bring along the American with "green marbles"—describing my eyes. I finally had my chance to get behind the walls of an Arab woman's life in a more traditional society than Egypt.

We gathered at a house in a residential neighborhood where, among just us girls, we could take off our *shaylas* and put them around our necks like scarves. That seemed to be a signal for the women to let their hair down in conversation, as well. They were obsessed with the politics of national reunification, worried that the antagonistic ideologies of the two Yemens might lead to civil war. They despised the Russian women in the South who wore shorts and sleeveless tops, even during Ramadan. *Haram!* One of the guests, who appeared to be in her sixties, pulled out a small handgun that she had kept hidden between her breasts and said she was ready in case any hostile moves came from the South. Others were more resigned to whatever fate had in store. "What to do?" one of them said—one of the set phrases that many of them could use in English. Another was: "This is the life."

It was hard to be too anxious with all the wonderful food laid out before us. As we discussed the dangers of the coming strategic upheaval we ate *sambusas,* the fried meat and vegetable dumplings known as *samosas* in India. The host also offered chicken meat on skewers, meatballs of lamb and chick-peas, stuffed grape leaves, soup, fresh bread, salads, tabouli, and all kinds of fruit and juices. It was wonderful. And I was delighted to find these women, so muted in public, almost exploding with ideas in the privacy of their homes.

Their husbands could not be any more intelligent than these women were, and these wives clearly could hold their own in any family discussions with the men. These women were well read, they had opinions, and they did not shy away from politics.

They were just as curious about me as I was about them. They asked if boys and girls really attended school together in the United States. I tried to explain the U.S. system, including the difference between public schools and private schools. We also have Catholic schools, I said—"and Jewish schools," one of the women interjected. Americans can practice any religion, I said, or no religion at all.

That point they could not understand. "How could you not have religion?" one said. America was so bountiful, so rich, so developed, peaceful, and calm, she said. "How could you not believe in God?" Most of us do, I said.

That faith would prove helpful sooner than I knew, as Saddam quietly prepared for his bold move into Kuwait. As I flew home from Yemen in my jeans, I had no idea that within weeks I would be flying back to the Arab peninsula in full battle gear, my weapon locked and loaded. Yemeni leaders would make a costly decision to support Saddam in his decision to invade Kuwait, losing U.S. financial and military support for years.

GULF WAR I

IN THE THIRTEEN YEARS SINCE I
had joined the Army, we had studied wars, planned for wars, and
built a great war machine. Then the real thing snuck up on us. In the
summer of 1991, the Third Army was taking part in a major joint
exercise with the Navy, Air Force, and Marines at Hurlburt Field in
the Florida panhandle. The scenario: an Iraqi invasion of Kuwait,
and how the United States would respond. As is common during
such exercises, the country we were practicing against grew slightly
paranoid. Saddam Hussein had already been quarreling with his
Arab neighbors, hectoring them to raise prices on oil exports. He
stepped up his confrontational rhetoric, and Iraqi troops did begin
massing on the border with Kuwait. We assumed it was his usual
bluster and bluff.

As a targeteer responsible for Iraq, among other countries, I was
in the thick of the action. I found myself attending briefings on exercise intelligence followed by briefings on real-world intelligence,
and it was getting harder to tell them apart. We had the surreal
sense of charging around Florida chasing the reflections of enemy
forces that were actually executing the operations we were simulat-

ing. You had to stay focused. Is this briefing real or part of the exercise? Most officers were taking the absurd situation lightheartedly. Occasionally somebody would say, "Oh, yeah, maybe he *will* cross the border"—never believing that Saddam actually would.

The Iraqi leader chose his moment carefully. If there is ever a time to catch the collective leadership of the Middle East napping or vacationing, August is it. And his forces moved into Kuwait just as the American exercise had concluded and we were all flying home. When we heard first reports of the Iraqi invasion back at Fort McPherson, we could hardly believe it. Maybe this was just a feint intended to show how serious Saddam was about his claim that Kuwait was a breakaway province of Iraq. Then Kuwaitis started dying, and Saddam's tanks rumbled onto Kuwaiti airfields, grounding Kuwait's small but tough air force. The reality hit us like a hammer: Our exercise had just come to life.

Third Army had a worldwide deployment mission. During times of war, we did not send troops into battle per se, but we served as the Army headquarters under Central Command, led at the time by General Norman Schwarzkopf. The regulars around Fort McPherson were in a state of mild shock: Third Army headquarters had not deployed since World War II, and now Schwarzkopf was telling them to be on the ground in Saudi Arabia within days. Third Army reservists, including me, were quickly mobilized, meaning we had to suspend our civilian lives and become full-time soldiers. I assumed we would hold the fort for the regulars stateside while they were carrying the fight to Saddam. Fort McPherson became a madhouse. Regulars were scrambling to deploy, civilian employees were confused, and reservists were swarming in to mobilize before the base was ready to accommodate them.

At one point the Third Army operations officer called me in des-

peration, asking if I could find some pagers to help the command
stay in touch with staff members after duty hours. In my civilian
role as director of security and operations for the base, I had a contract for pagers with an Atlanta company. With one phone call, I
was able to come up with twenty-four activated pagers instantly
and a guarantee that we could have as many as we needed within
three days. The ops officer was mightily pleased to have a solution
to a problem that had stumped his uniformed staff members. "If we
deploy," he said, "you're on the same damn aircraft as me."

Sure enough, the order came. Since George was still in Yemen, I
had to arrange all the details of a hasty getaway. The next day I got
my shots, updated my will, sent my parrot, Casey, off to my brother
in New Jersey, and talked a friend into house-sitting while I was gone.

Three days after Saddam invaded Kuwait, I was flying to Saudi
Arabia with the Third Army's jump TOC (tactical operations center).
I later discovered that I was one of the very first reservists deployed.
Third Army had to establish its presence immediately to help set up
Operation Desert Shield, deterring Saddam from continuing his
march through Kuwait into the Saudi oil fields. And Schwarzkopf's
plan for an eventual counterstrike called for a massive air campaign
against Iraq before the ground war began, requiring targeteers like
me to get to work ASAP.

Our C-141 transport plane stopped for a few hours in the Azores,
where hundreds of U.S. soldiers were sleeping on cots set up in
hangars, waiting for the next leg of their deployment. We timed our
own flight to arrive in Riyadh just after midnight in blackout conditions. But something was wrong. The atmosphere inside the plane
grew tense after our pilots reported that they could not communicate with the Saudi airfield. There was some fear that Saddam had
moved faster than anticipated. Could Iraqi troops already be in con-

trol of the airfield? Were we fifty officers and soldiers—specialists in transportation, logistics, operations, and administration—about to find ourselves facing the front edge of the Iraqi army?

We were already in battle gear, ready for whatever awaited us on the airfield. The aircraft commander told us to lock and load a magazine into our weapons, and all you could hear was the sharp click of magazines shoved into the wells of M16 rifles. Riyadh and the airfield were blanketed in darkness, as was the interior of our airplane. I was trying without success to see the other soldiers' faces. I was going to remember this flight. People around me were whispering, "Karpinski, are you all right?" And I was whispering back, "Yeah, I'm fine"—though it was unclear why we were all whispering over the roar of the engines. We made a bumpy instrument landing, and the pilot continued his commentary: We still had no communications contact; there was probably some problem on the Saudi side; we can't confirm who's in charge of the airfield. The aircraft finally stopped and shut down its engines. The door opened, and the silhouette of a man appeared. "Welcome to Riyadh," he said, "and I bet you're all glad I'm speaking English."

He was an Army major stationed in Riyadh as part of the training detachment. The air base had been enforcing not only a blackout, it turned out, but radio silence. We felt like jumping on him as if he had just scored the winning touchdown. "The first thing I want you to do is take the magazines out of your weapons and put them on safe," he said. "Nobody needs to get shot."

Nerves and adrenaline got me precisely as far as I had to go. We checked into the Marriott Hotel in Riyadh at about 3:00 A.M. and were accommodated six to a room. I managed to make it to one of the beds before collapsing. Two days later Schwarzkopf ordered us out of the hotel, which he deemed too vulnerable to a terrorist attack. We moved into the basement parking garage of the Saudi ministry of defense, a building with an elaborate protective façade that looked like the work of bees so we dubbed it "the honeycomb building."

George had to make his own getaway from Yemen. When the Yemenis sided with Saddam, the United States quickly drew down its presence in the country. George helped evacuate diplomats and their families, then departed himself for Saudi Arabia. But we did not get to fight the war together. By the time he landed in Riyadh, I had been sent off on an assignment to Abu Dhabi. And by the time I returned to Riyadh, George had been sent back to the States to attend the command and general staff college.

My first responsibility in Riyadh was to help set up shop and launch into our mission. I later learned that I was one of the first women ever to set foot in the ministry of defense headquarters. I had a challenging job. We had to manage logistics for the hundreds of thousands of troops bearing down on Saudi Arabia, while also laying groundwork for the powerful military thrust into Iraq that lay ahead. We worked almost non-stop with protective masks and atropine injections by our side in case Saddam decided to launch chemical attacks.

We were very conscious of that contingency. As our showdown with the Iraqi leader intensified, he fired Scud missiles at Riyadh— you could see them flying in—and we feared that some of them were equipped with chemical warheads. When the alarms sounded, we had to put on our protective masks and wait. I was worried about Saddam's weapons of mass destruction, but I was just as hung up about the antidote: the atropine we would have to self-administer. You were supposed to slam the auto-injector into your thigh, sending a needle 2 inches deep into your flesh. You were supposed to just leave it there—don't worry, it will fall out by itself, they told us— while preparing the next injection. I practiced this in my head. I didn't mind getting shots, but I had a phobia about jamming this thing into my thigh. I told our chemical NCO, "I don't think I will be able to do this, I really don't."

"Believe me," he said, "if there's a real attack you'll be able to do it."

"Well, if I can't, will you do it for me?" I beseeched him. "When those alarms go off, I'm coming right over beside you." Thankfully, I never had to test my shaky resolve—or his willingness to cooperate.

In any case, we had little time to worry about Saddam's Scud missiles and their possible payloads. We all had to develop ambidexterity, doing several jobs at once. The lieutenant colonel in charge of civil affairs divided his time between winning the hearts and minds of the locals and intimidating the enemy. He even developed propaganda in the form of milk cartons for delivery throughout Kuwait that bore messages warning Iraqis to surrender before the full weight of the American military machine descended upon them. For my part, I kept tabs on arriving ships, learning the workings of "ro-ro's" (roll-on/roll-off supply ships), "ro-lo's" (roll-on/lift-off), and others while at the same time working to identify Iraqi targets, just in case the milk cartons didn't work.

General Schwarzkopf was operating under the philosophy of Colin Powell, chairman of the joint chiefs of staff at the time. The Powell doctrine called for answering any military challenge with overwhelming force—enough troops, firepower, supplies, and hardware to blow away the enemy. In one case, logisticians bumped three Special Forces A Teams that were scheduled to fly to the battle zone in order to use their plane to ship over a piece of hardware they considered more important: a component for a Patriot antimissile battery. The priority would have been completely different today, under Defense Secretary Donald Rumsfeld. He believes in smaller, more maneuverable, more lethal fighting forces. In Rumsfeld's scheme, each Special Forces soldier is worth about fifty regular soldiers; if it were up to him, the whole Army would consist of Special Forces. I don't completely disagree with that vision, but having managed personnel issues in the Army—and married someone who became a Special Forces officer—I have a hard time seeing it actually happen. It takes a special person to join the Special Forces. It's best to be spectacularly fit, brilliant, multi-lingual, somewhat suicidal, and ready to fly anywhere at a moment's notice. It's hard to be a Special Forces soldier and also have a credit card, bank account, cat, bird, or spouse. It will be no easy challenge for Rumsfeld to find enough people like that to fill up an entire Army.

Schwarzkopf had set aside a lot of time for the air war and a lot of ordinance, including the "smartest," most precise weapons America had ever used in war. These required painstaking target selection. It wasn't as simple as targeting a bridge to complicate Saddam's troop movements. We had to target the bridge while identifying and safeguarding the oil pipeline that ran beside it. Our mission was to punish the Iraqi dictator without punishing his people; we wanted to drive Saddam out of Kuwait without crippling Iraq to the point of a humanitarian disaster. We had to target buildings just as precisely, leaving facilities such as schools and hospitals untouched—unless we were convinced that Saddam was using them as weapons depots instead of for their intended purposes. Our warplanes could blow away anything we selected, so we had to use our best intelligence to select correctly and wisely.

Meanwhile, we were also working to pave the way for the multinational force of ground soldiers gathering from around the world for the assault on Saddam's forces. I kept close watch on the list of arriving U.S. units and noted one in particular: the 82nd Airborne, including my brother Jay, a non-commissioned officer in one of the brigades. He and his comrades in the division, who affectionately

called him "Moonbeam," had landed in Dhahran on their way to
the Kuwait border. Jay had arrived on August 25, a day before his
birthday, so I found a courier who was on his way to Dhahran and
asked him to deliver a birthday box of cigarettes, gum, playing
cards, and other goodies I had put together. My brother was pleas-
antly surprised, though he almost took the courier's head off when
the guy came up to him and said, "Hey, are you Moonbeam?"

The pressure and workload were enormous. My journey of cultural discovery in the Middle East had to wait as I devoted my few
hours off duty to the search for sleep. Before long I discovered the
luxuries of the American Embassy, with its swimming pool and
showers. After a tense night of work, I would attend the DARF conference—planning our daily aerial and reconnaissance flights—grab
a bus to the embassy, take a reclining chair under a beach umbrella
by the pool and sleep for a few hours. Then I would get up, take a
shower, and head back to work.

Our official quarters, in the parking garage of the honeycomb
building, were less pleasant but more convenient, located across the
street from where we worked. We had cots and a mess operation,
and soldiers had draped tent canvases over cables to give us seventeen women some privacy. Men could use bathrooms on any floor of
the defense headquarters, while facilities were reserved for women
on the fourth and fifth floors. Saudi men regularly barged into our
bathrooms, unable to conceive of the idea of a ladies' room in their
military center, so we found it wise to station a guard outside while
we were using the rooms, especially if we were taking showers. This
was a routine part of military life for a woman. When we dropped
our guard, we sometimes paid for it. During our Florida exercises,
two men wrapped their heads and bodies in towels the way women
do and strolled through the women's shower tent, got a good look,

and shouted, "Have a great day, ladies" on their way out. Usually we were more vigilant. During field exercises, my pal, Captain Vicky Nellis, and I would take turns guarding the latrine for each other. In Saudi Arabia I would grab a passerby in uniform and say, "Just stand there for a minute," while I went in and took a shower.

It was too hot to run outside in the sun in the morning after work, so some of us discovered that the north and west wall in a vacant section of our parking garage—we called it the "backward 7"—would make an adequate running track. Somebody calculated that if you ran up, across, and back twenty-three times, you had gone 2 miles. It was still hot, and airless, but at least it shielded us from the sun.

Credit the Saudis with trying to accommodate American servicewomen, not always with the best results. After my shift one morning I missed the bus to the embassy, so I descended into the parking garage to sleep on my cot. I took off the outer shirt of my "chocolate chips"—what we called our desert camouflage uniforms because that's what the pattern resembled—leaving my T-shirt on. I also managed to unlace my boots, but fell deeply asleep before I could take them off. I dreamed I heard a car running and was shouting for it to stop. Finally I woke up enough to figure out that I was not dreaming. I pushed myself onto my elbows and saw a small Datsun pickup truck making its way into our midst, full of Pakistani workers and equipment. The workers had come to put in shower stalls, a gesture by the Saudi authorities to make life easier for us. But nobody told the workers that they would be driving into the midst of twelve or fifteen American women, some wearing just bras and panties, some stark naked, some sleeping obliviously on their cots. The Pakistanis stood there staring as if they had died and gone to heaven. I started shouting, "First Sergeant! First Sergeant!"

He was on the other side of the canvas wall. "Ma'am?" he called back with obvious concern in his voice. "Ma'am? Is that you? Are you okay?"

"There's men in here!" I shouted back. "Men in here!"

"Ma'am, ma'am, can I come in?" the first sergeant asked.

"Why not?" I answered. "Everybody else seems to be in here. Get these guys out!"

He escorted the workers out as discreetly as possible while women grabbed for T-shirts and covered those who remained asleep through it all.

Sleep was a valued commodity. Our vanguard staff essentially was on call 24/7, working out problems we had never anticipated, fielding assignments for which we had never been trained. Never before had I worked so closely and smoothly with people from all of the services, as well as Saudi officers and Japanese allies, among others. As our military buildup continued, reinforcements flowed into our headquarters staff and the work load became more manageable—and less exciting. The air war was ready to go. The troops were on the ground, training for their charge across the border. And the responsibilities of those who had helped put it all in place were easing. We missed the daily adrenaline rush, but the Army didn't forget us. I was awarded a bronze star for my role in Operation Desert Shield, a lifelong reminder of the drama of creating an overwhelming force from nothing in the middle of nowhere.

•   •   •

JUST AS THE GROUND WAR WAS ABOUT TO begin, my boss called me down to his office and told me I was on

the short list of female officers being considered for a different, classified assignment.

"Is it in Riyadh?" I asked.

"No, actually, it's not," he said.

"Then I'm interested," I said.

My assignment turned out to be 480 miles away in the United
Arab Emirates, the federation of seven Persian Gulf sheikhdoms located across Saudi Arabia's southeastern border. I had to look on a
map to see where the UAE was. To get there I had to venture into
the Saudi civilian world, a task that always had implications for a
woman's dress code. On duty in Riyadh, walking across the street
from where I lived to where I worked, I could wear my Army uniform—if I rolled down my sleeves, turned up my collar, clamped
my hat down to my eyebrows, and had a man accompany me. But
any time I strayed into the larger city I had to wear a veil or risk the
wrath of the *muttawa* and their canes. I was well covered up when I
went to the airport, talking my way past guards and immigration
agents, often getting my veil stuck in my mouth. The whole cha-
rade was irritating. You know I'm an American soldier, I thought.
Let me out of this cloak.

When I arrived in Abu Dhabi, the UAE capital, I saw women
with their heads uncovered and left my Saudi gear in my bag. The
place didn't look like much at night: sand, a few streetlights, non-
descript buildings. When I awoke in my hotel room the next
morning, covered in clean, fresh cotton sheets, I couldn't imagine
where I was. I must have forgotten to take the atropine, died from
a chemical attack, and gone to my reward. I looked out the window and saw the brilliant, turquoise waters of the Persian Gulf—
further confirmation that I had left the world as I knew it. I had
been given two weeks in this paradise, working out of the U.S.

Embassy, meeting Saudi princes and potentates late at night over thick coffee.

My job was to evaluate an extraordinary idea: to establish a women's military training program in the United Arab Emirates. The president's wife, a charismatic figure in her own right, apparently had been inundated with requests from UAE women wanting to do something, anything, to protect their country should Saddam be stupid enough to bring the war there. It was exhilarating even to consider this opportunity for Arab women; no other Gulf country had women trained to be part of the military force. My doubts were swept away after only two days of talks. The ruling hierarchy was solidly behind this idea, and how could it fail with the president's wife leading the charge?

Like the rest of the Arabian peninsula, the UAE was obsessed by security worries. Abu Dhabi lay only slightly farther away from Saddam's missiles than did Riyadh. The women I met kept asking, "Will he come here? Why is Saddam doing this? What will we do?" Iraqis were their Arab brothers, and the two societies had lived together in relative peace for many years. Emirati women had married Iraqis, had lived in Iraq or at least traveled there. Why was Saddam betraying them?

We gathered a group of young women together in an assembly hall. Any city has what the military calls critical facilities, I told them: broadcast towers, water systems, power plants, and the like. But in a war, men in the UAE army might have to leave home and go to Kuwait to fight, or to Iraq. At those words, the women in the room gasped. It was a frightening new idea to them: Their men in uniform might actually have to fight.

If that happened, I said, who would be left to guard the UAE's critical facilities? Then I answered my own question: You could serve in vital support roles. Women could join the army.

The country was ready for change. The UAE was no Lebanon or Egypt, but its society was more open by degrees than Saudi Arabia's. In Abu Dhabi, most women showed their faces to the world, and you could see them driving to work or school. Emiratis also could see social problems arising in Saudi Arabia: alienated young people growing impatient for social change or descending into religious fanaticism. The UAE's leaders wanted no such trends to develop in their own little sheikhdoms. They realized that opening up more opportunities was the best way to relieve the pressure, and the Army could help. The ultimate decision maker was the UAE's president, Sheikh Zayed bin Sultan al Nahyan, but the real impetus came from Sheikh Zayed's second and favorite wife (he had four at a time), Sheikha Fatima bint Mubarak. As head of the UAE's Women's Federation, she saw the terrible deprivation of women who came to the organization for aid, and she whispered into the ear of her son, Sheikh Mohammed bin Zayed al Nahyan, the armed forces chief of staff. Sheikh Mohammed, in turn, approached U.S. Ambassador Edward S. Walker and the U.S. military attaché, Colonel Jack McGuinness, asking whether the United States might agree to train a contingent of women soldiers. McGuinness sent a message to the Pentagon. A short list of potential trainers emerged, and I ended up with the prize: a two-week trip to the UAE to develop a plan for the Emiratis.

During that time we stitched together the outlines of a training program that would integrate women into the UAE army. "This is a great opportunity for the women of this country," I told the U.S. ambassador and the crown prince during one meeting. "They're going to show you what they can do."

OUR VERY OWN CHOCOLATE CHIPS

MY INTEREST IN THE MIDDLE
East had always been personal, not professional. I tended to believe
those who told me that I could visit the region but could never work
there as a military woman—and would never want to live like a
ghost under a veil. But now here I was, in the cultural hinterland of
Arabia, listening to a government under the sway of a very powerful woman asking me to help integrate women into an Arab army.
That was one invitation I would never turn down. I thought I would
spend two weeks in the UAE; all told I ended up spending six years.

There were compelling reasons pushing the UAE toward this
revolutionary development, motives that went far beyond any
growing fondness for women's rights. After seeing what had happened to Kuwait, the Emiratis were feeling particularly vulnerable
and really did believe that women could play the traditional role of
American WACs, keeping the home fires burning if the men had to
go to war. The UAE's standing army, filled with foreign conscripts
and haphazardly trained, needed whatever help it could get. In any
case, even if peace continued to reign in the Emirates, the country
needed more economic options for its women.

125

Older Emiratis could remember a time before the oil flowed, when even electricity was scarce; in Abu Dhabi, the old-timers reminisced, people would gather on the beach at night to play cards by the light of oil lamps. Now that the wealth had arrived, not everybody benefited equally. Ras al Khaimah and other smaller emirates in the federation fell short of the prosperity enjoyed by Abu Dhabi and Dubai. Women in these poorer emirates—and across the country, to some extent—were disproportionately worse off, especially if they were still single past the prime marrying age of fourteen to eighteen. Not every single woman in her twenties was considered a loser; in some cases, parents were too liberal to push their daughters out the door or too wealthy to need a dowry from a husband's family. But many young, single women were indeed social cripples. They had failed to snare a husband, or they had been divorced and sent back to their families, sometimes with children to support. And on their own, they looked forward to a life of dismal prospects.

These hard-luck, unmarried women were often educated. Many had college degrees. They were qualified to work in banks, schools, hospitals, and offices. But they frequently faced hopeless discrimination. In a more traditional place like Ras al Khaimah, especially, a banker might have two applicants: a woman with an accounting degree from college and a man with a seventh-grade education. Who got the job? The man, without doubt. It was the right thing to do, according to conventional reasoning. He had a family to support, while the woman just wanted money to spend on makeup and magazines.

As a result of these attitudes, women were underused in a little country that needed to mobilize all of its resources. The UAE did occasionally invest in single women who showed exceptional talent and intelligence. An Emirati friend of mine, Hessa, was married and divorced in her teens, a plight that ordinarily would eliminate the possibility of a college scholarship in the United States. She applied for one anyway and was turned down by the UAE minister of education. But she pressed her case, pointing out her top honors in mathematics, her aptitude for engineering, and her good sense in escaping a bad marriage. The government finally relented, sending Hessa on a full scholarship to the University of Toledo, in Ohio, where she earned a degree in civil engineering. She returned to the UAE to work for her father's construction company and also took a position in the national department of public works, where she served as one of the few formally trained engineers. After an Emirati woman had seen Toledo—including the freedoms of women there—it was hard to return to Arabia and life as a second-class citizen.

After a week of research, I wrote a design for a boot camp with heavy emphasis on physical training, patrolling, guard duty, and weapons use. I gave it to Colonel McGuinness, the U.S. military attaché, waited a day, then was summoned to a midnight meeting with Sheikh Mohammed and Mohammed Saeed al Badi, the UAE secretary of defense. The conversation circled around toward the subject of my report. "It's a very good report," Sheikh Mohammed said noncommittally. Then he stood up and announced that I should come with him. My first inclination was to back away, wondering where we might be going. "I want you to meet someone," he insisted, instructing everybody else to stay where they were.

We drove to a modest building that reminded me of a Girl Scout retreat. It was part of a small, rustic compound in a fairly isolated place. Women of different ages relaxed in small groups, drinking coffee and tea or working on crafts. Sheikh Mohammed took me to what appeared to be a plainly furnished office, until I saw that the simple furniture all was made of fine teak, clean and perfectly polished. I realized we had come to the women's federation, and I was about to meet his mother, Sheikha Fatima, wife of the UAE president. He approached a woman wearing the typical black *abaya* and *shayla*, her hands decorated with henna. He kissed her gently and she held him tenderly—the genuine, loving embrace of a mother who had not seen her son all day.

"I want you to meet Major Janis," he said. Sheikha Fatima greeted me politely, taking my hand in hers. She picked up a *Newsweek* whose cover showed a picture of a female American soldier wearing a desert camouflage uniform and a maroon beret. She told me she wanted her girls to wear chocolate chips just like that. She suggested several amendments to my program and gave her approval casually, changing the future of her country and my life in the space of less than twenty minutes.

I spent a few days in the UAE inspecting facilities, meeting people who would be working with me and speaking to excited groups of young women. At first they were frightened for their security when the United States launched its land war. Then, when the war ended in 100 hours, they were afraid that we might cancel plans to create a women's military unit for them.

Sheikha Fatima was not going to let that happen. Before I flew back to Riyadh after my exploratory trip, she threw a reception for me at one of the royal palaces, apparently concerned that our first meeting had been too perfunctory. If her goal was to impress me, she succeeded within the first thirty seconds. Hessa came with me, and heavily armed security guards escorted us to the function. Sheikha Fatima greeted us in the ballroom of her main palace, a round chamber fitted perfectly with a rich Persian carpet. Silk brocades hung from the walls, and alcoves displayed Moroccan furniture inlaid with teak patterns and mother of pearl. The room was furnished in lavish French provincial style, the chairs and couches heavily gilded. Sheikha Fatima wore an elegant long dress with ornate gold stitching in the Moroccan style. Hessa introduced me to about 100 guests—all women—while a women's musical ensemble played softly in the background. The fragrant smoke of burning *oud* wood filled the air, the quintessential Arab scent.

I sat next to Sheikha Fatima, who often took my hand as we talked. I wore a long dress and pulled my hair back, but my fair features had the usual effect. Through Hessa, who served as our interpreter, Sheikha Fatima told me that my eyes were something from God; she said she could see in my eyes that I wanted to make this program possible for the women of the United Arab Emirates. Tea arrived, along with caviar, tabouli, small skewers of lamb, and perfect samples of local fruit. As Sheikha Fatima prepared a serving of caviar for me, I had to explain that I was allergic to eggs, one of the condiments. She immediately ordered the removal of the caviar and directed the servants to deliver a generous new portion without the egg garnishment.

The women were as informed and curious as those I had met in Yemen. They asked me about Saddam's motives and the repercussions of the war. Many were excited, sensing that a glass ceiling was shattering, proclaiming that the war would give Arab women a chance to show what they could do. They exalted the women of Kuwait, who had replaced killed or captured men in the underground, passing information to the Americans, hiding fugitives, and assisting the liberation forces any way they could. If the Kuwaitis needed help, these elegant Emirati women vowed to answer the call. And they were ready to defend their own homeland, as a kind of civil defense force. Women in their forties asked if our new program could teach them how to shoot guns on the rifle ranges we would build. At that point, Sheikha Fatima calmed them all down. First we must establish the women's military force, she said. Then we can talk about teaching women to shoot guns.

"Could women in the UAE really do this?" someone asked me. "Absolutely," I answered. "I'm listening to all this here tonight, all this excitement, and I know if you have sisters or daughters or nieces or female friends, you are going to encourage them to do this."

"Yes," they agreed excitedly. "Yes!" I could tell that they now would all go home and sell their husbands on this idea.

After the appetizers came a selection of sweets, more fragrant wood, and trays of perfumes. Everybody took long, crystal sticks from the perfume bottles and touched the scents to their arms, necks, and clothing—getting all perfumed up to go home to their mates or, in my case, to the Hilton Hotel. The next day I received a package from Sheikha Fatima and opened it to find a stunning, floor-length green dress that fit me perfectly. She must have been sizing me up in more ways than one. The note, in lovely Arabic, said: "This will always match the color of your eyes. You will remember the United Arab Emirates."

• • •

IN RIYADH, THE VICTORIOUS COALITION WAS preparing to dismantle its overwhelming force and go home. I flew back to the United States after my exploratory two weeks in the United Arab Emirates in a predictable funk. The adrenaline rush of war planning was gone, as was my life of high diplomacy and creative soldiering in the UAE. A lot of other Gulf war veterans felt the same way. We returned from Desert Storm to cheers and parades, then had to get our feet back on the ground in a more humdrum world, assigned to mundane jobs, writing the kind of after-action reports that nobody ever reads. But just as I was settling back into my routine with the Third Army, I received a call from our embassy in the UAE: They wanted me back. The U.S. Army major who had replaced me in the training program had not worked out, and Sheikha Fatima was saying that only Major Janis would do. I received a generous contract offer by mail, and once again the Third Army allowed me to deploy as a military adviser and let me keep my military service on track, including promotions. Only a woman could train female recruits in an Arab country, and in me the UAE leaders believed they had a woman who could teach military skills as well as convey military pride and discipline.

I caught a flight back to Fort Bragg, where my all-woman UAE training team—a major and nine non-commissioned officers—already had been assembled. The women in my team had been chosen individually by their commands, and they were all first-rate. They amounted to an all-woman A-Team, with specialists in signal, medical, chemical, police, and other branches. The NCOs virtually all had been drill sergeants, and they were all such proven leaders that I feared they would blow the roof off the building competing with each other. But I didn't have to worry. These women were hungry for the mission and were committed to making it a success.

None of them ever had been to the Middle East, so I began with the down and dirty. They would have to wear long-sleeved shirts and trousers when they were out of uniform. They could not smoke in public or on our training grounds. Alcohol was available by ration card at the U.S. Embassy, but none could be consumed at our boot camp. "This is a program that is going to change the culture," I told them, "and the only thing that will defeat this program is if they detect any influence that they consider negative—smoking, drinking, miniskirts, rude behavior . . ." Then there were the Arab male trainers they would meet in our program. They are ultra-conservative, I warned the women. They won't shake a woman's hand, including yours. They won't allow themselves to be in a room alone with you. They might smoke in your presence, but you may not smoke in theirs. All these sacrifices will seem negligible, I said, when you discover the enthusiasm and commitment of the Arab women we'll be training.

When we arrived in the UAE, I gave our team an orientation tour of the Emirates, from north to south, poor to rich. Then we set up our training center and waited for the first recruits to our four-month program. The Emirates called our school the Khawla bint Al Azwar Military School for Women, after a brave female Muslim warrior who had fought alongside the Prophet Mohammed (peace be upon him). The army had received more than 3,000 applicants, interviewed more than 1,200, selected 800, and ultimately delivered 180 young women by bus to our camp. After the first week, that number dropped to 130 as the realities of military training set in. You want me to get up at *what* time in the morning? You want me to clean *what*?

As the recruits arrived in their long dresses and perfume, our drill sergeants met them at the busses, conveying their orders clearly even if they were shouting in English. Within a few days, the instructors identified the recruits who could understand enough English to interpret, and the instructors themselves had picked up a few key Arabic commands. We issued three sets of T-shirts—some red, some white, and some green—so that when the women marched in their black sweat pants they showed all the colors of the UAE flag. After a few days their camouflage uniforms arrived, and the women marched proudly in their chocolate chips—looking as sharp as any American soldier on the cover of *Newsweek*.

We insisted on the highest standards of training. The training program for male recruits in the UAE army was designed mainly to acclimate them to the disciplines of soldiers in uniform. Their physical training demands were modest (possibly because their instructors were not in great shape), and they received no weapons training until they reported to their unit, and then only if it was a combat unit. By contrast, we put our women through rigorous physical training. We had no choice: We had to give them a military mind-set. Many had grown up spoiled by servants, came in overweight, and had to work themselves into good enough shape to march. We banned cigarettes, strictly rationed chocolate, and forbade them to use telephones at the camp for the first two weeks. After that, each woman could make one five-minute phone call home as a drill sergeant kept time with a stopwatch. By the end of four months, our recruits' drill and ceremony performance was excellent, as was their marksmanship and ability to maintain their weapons. We gave them classroom training on the history of their country and of the UAE armed forces. When we asked what happened in 1991, nobody had trouble remembering the answer. "We changed the military!" they would shout.

I knew we had made the program work. I could see it at our first graduation ceremony. When the graduates demonstrated their ability to break down an M16 and put it back together within 12 seconds—blindfolded—their fathers and brothers were stunned. "She's my daughter!" parents cried over and over. Our soldiers efficiently put on and took off their chemical masks. They ran an obstacle course, nimbly crawling under some obstacles and jumping over others. All that and they could also demonstrate new mastery of word-processing skills on our classroom computers. Family members kissed our hands for sending back young women who made their beds without prompting and used their time well all day.

Our main challenge came after graduation: We had to find jobs for our soldiers in an army that had never accommodated women. We kept about twenty of our best soldiers to help train the next class and sent the others to learn practical skills as administrative workers, communicators, and military police officers, among other specialties. Still, most commanders didn't want them. They thought women would upset the harmony and efficiency of their offices. I went to Sheikh Mohammed to explain the problem, and he said simply, "Leave this with me." A couple of days later, commanders were flooding the school with telephone calls asking for our graduates to be assigned to their units.

That still didn't mean our young women were entirely welcome. Our soldiers continued to use the school as their dormitory, heading off to their assignments at 8:00 in the morning—after PT—and working straight through until 2:00 in the afternoon, when buses would bring them back. We put them in tan dress uniforms: jackets that came to mid-thigh length over trousers or long skirts, topped off by their berets and *shaylas*. We inspected them every day before work and made sure we sent them off looking sharp.

At first, they were regarded as a novelty. They were kept segregated from the men, working in separate offices or behind dividing walls—taking any possibility of disruptions or sexual harassment out of the equation. When our women came back at night, they had stories of men treating them gingerly but politely. The telephone operators would giggle about the silence that often greeted them when they answered a call: The speechless man on the other end simply could not comprehend the idea of a woman answering a military phone. The young women knew they were changing history. "Ma'am, ma'am!" they would shout as they got off the busses after returning from work. "You won't believe what happened today!"

Their workload increased steadily, and a month into our second class, commanders were calling the head of our school, Colonel Jumah Rashid Saif al Dhaheri, asking for as many female soldiers as he could supply. Our women dressed like professionals, used perfect military etiquette, understood the national culture better than many of the foreign male soldiers, and were 100 percent dedicated.

If there were still any whispered complaints about putting women in the Army, they were silenced by the UAE president himself. A few months after our young women joined the Army, we asked if they could participate in the national-day parade. The organizers said no, so once again I went to Sheikh Mohammed, the military chief of staff, who once again said, "Leave this with me." Sure enough, we soon found ourselves drilling our women for their opportunity to march past a roster of the nation's dignitaries led by the president, Sheikh Zayed. They looked so sharp, marched so crisply to the commands of the drum major, Afra Ali al Niyadi, held themselves so proudly for all the world to see that I was almost in tears. As they passed the president in review, Sheikh Zayed rose to his feet, laughing and cheering—and so, immediately, did every other dignitary in sight, applauding the new era that was passing before them.

GET ME AN AIRPLANE,
I'M GOING TO IRAQ

I ENDED UP SPENDING THE NEXT five years in the UAE—until 1997—guiding more than a thousand women through basic training and ensuring that my program and their service became part of the UAE military culture. After a couple of years in Abu Dhabi, I was reclassified as an inactive Reserve officer, a status that let me work indefinitely in the Middle East while keeping my U.S. military career on track. Back in the States I had enrolled in the command and general staff college, and was able to continue my course requirements in Abu Dhabi by correspondence. After I had completed half the requirements, I received notification by letter that I had been selected for promotion to lieutenant colonel. (I completed the remaining half of the course upon return to the States.)

An ambitious officer climbing through the ranks does not enjoy a gentler incline in the Reserves. But I had certain advantages over other Reserve officers. I had had ten years in the regular Army, where I had earned qualifications as an MP, jump master, and senior parachutist. I wore a combat patch on my right arm and had earned a bronze star from Desert Storm. I had held a diplomatic post in the

UAE. And I broke a lot of the preconceptions about women in the military. They can't do PT? Look at my scores. They can't serve as the commander of troops for general officer ceremonies? Watch me. They don't take the tough jobs? Look at the command positions I had held. On top of all that, women were flooding into the Army Reserve. In every one of the units I commanded in my later career, about one in every four soldiers was a woman; the proportion may have reached 40 percent in some of the headquarters units. In the circumstances, the Reserve command was trying its best to find competent female leaders.

In short, it was a very good time to be a woman in the Reserves. In the regular Army, the women arriving from West Point and the other academies were still working their way through the lower ranks; that macho, male officer clubiness still prevailed in the senior leadership. But in the Reserves, women saw opportunities for advancement opening up. We were breaking down walls all over the place, and a lot of men were willing to support our efforts. If you were a woman who wanted to advance in the Army, a reservist is what you wanted to be.

When I finally did return home from the Middle East, tan and fit, both my civilian and military careers seemed to be taking off. In the Emirates I had taken advantage of my civilian experience in business and administration and spent my spare time teaching business classes for Boston University and other American institutions that had satellite operations there. I also discovered that I could play a role as a consultant, helping Emirati businessmen negotiate fair deals with their U.S. partners. When I got back to the States, I developed corporate improvement programs and ways to help companies evaluate their personnel. Before long, my client list stretched from Colorado to Switzerland to Zimbabwe. George spent most of this period in the Middle East, running military advisory programs in Saudi Arabia,

Oman, and Jordan. We would find our islands of time together where and when we could—flying from Riyadh and Florida to meet in South Africa, for example.

I also rejoined the active Reserves—the weekend warriors—and applied for a challenging battalion command. I was named commander of the 160th MP battalion in Tallahassee, Florida. My new outfit was subordinate to the 3220th Garrison Support Unit, located in West Palm Beach, Florida. (Eventually we would end up in the 641st Area Support Group, out of St. Petersburg.) I had landed a great job, but I went back to the MP branch with some trepidation. Life might be improving for military women, but the MPs still included a lot of macho men. I could almost feel the questions that were being asked behind my back. How did a female get selected for battalion command over male officers? Were they pressured to select a female? Colonel Steve Read, commander of the 3220th and president of the selection board, took the pressure off me at the support command's first meeting of new battalion leaders in West Palm Beach. "We can't make board actions public," he told the group, "but I want you to know that the people who were chosen were the best and had the strongest files of everybody who applied, *without exception*." I appreciated those remarks enormously.

Steve Read became a two-star general and went on to head the Reserves' Readiness Command. After my troubles in Baghdad, he was one of only two general officers brave enough to call me, welcome me home, and thank me for my service. That remains true to the day I write this. I heard from longtime friends and hundreds of soldiers after I returned home, but not a single word from former colleagues, who must have been concerned about the fallout any contact with Janis Karpinski might have on their own careers.

As usual, I loved being in command. I was given a battalion of about 500 people in Tallahassee, Florida, where drill weekends in the past often had revolved around reading soldier magazines, taking three-hour lunches, and playing golf. George and I had purchased a home in Hilton Head, South Carolina, and I liked golf as much as anybody, but on my drill weekends, we emphasized physical training and military maneuvers. We had to prepare for war, I told my troops, because as we veterans of Desert Storm had learned, reservists in this day and age can find themselves flying off very quickly to serve in a place that's hard to find on a map. I kept my door open, always talked to the rank-and-file soldiers, and remembered the importance of their welfare. On one exercise, the NCOs took us on a shortcut along an unimproved road that blasted dust on our soldiers riding in open trucks. My driver pointed out that the soldiers were choking while their NCOs sat comfortably in the truck cabs. I blasted the NCOs myself that night: They had to get off their ego trips and think about how their actions were affecting the soldiers under their command.

I selected the operations officer, a rather conservative, highly competent major named Walt Mitchell, to be my number-two, the battalion's executive officer. Another officer later complained to me privately about this choice. This was Florida, he said, and Walt was black; people would put down our battalion if we had a black man in a position of authority. I told him that I disagreed, and that if I encountered any hint of discrimination, from him or anyone else, I would deal with it firmly. End of discussion.

Walt did a great job, especially teaching soldiers how to conduct prisoner-of-war operations, and we ended up becoming great friends. He followed me to my next command, and we both moved up the ladder. By the time I was a general, commanding a brigade in Baghdad, he was a colonel entering the war college. We had always kept in touch, and I hoped to bring him to Baghdad to help supervise our EPW (enemy prisoner of war) operations. Different as we were, we were also kindred spirits, facing down discrimination to rise through the military ranks. Neither of us was a member of the old-boys' network. We were both bustin' screws out, as we used to say. Then tragedy struck. On July 17, 2003, Walt was mowing the grass of his house in Florida when his mower hit a wasps' nest. He was stung more than seventy times, went into shock, and died. His wife, Jeanette, was devastated, and so was I, especially since I could not make it home for his funeral. I had been in Baghdad for less than a month, and the Army allows emergency leave only for the funeral of a family member.

I also became friends with the commander of our sister battalion in Tallahassee, Jim Payne. I was the new kid on the block, and Jim took it upon himself to help me out, giving me a lot of good tips. We did have different leadership styles. He was senior to me by a couple of years and one of those reservists who always managed to make the military work for him. If a drill weekend was scheduled when Florida State had a home football game, he would postpone it so soldiers could attend the game. He did not extend the same benefit to fans of Florida A&M, a traditionally black university, a policy that attracted criticism from the Army inspector general. But Jim didn't seem to care for rules. If the rule said don't smoke in a federal building, Jim would ignore it. When the boss came by, smelled smoke, and gave Jim a reprimand, Jim kept smoking. He got a second reprimand and still kept smoking. He got away with it. And he never deployed to a war zone. By the time the Iraq war came along, Jim was commanding the 300th MP brigade out of Inkster, Michigan. My brigade went to Baghdad, and Jim's went to Guantanamo Bay.

In St. Petersburg, our new brigade commander, Colonel Hughes Turner, a tall, intelligent Atlantan with a law degree who looked the model of an Army officer, took Jim Payne as his number-two, and Jim recommended me as operations officer. I had been in command only about eighteen months and was reluctant to take a less stimulating staff job, but it was part of the cycle between command and staff positions that earns promotions. The idea is that an officer should take the lessons learned in the field and apply them to the policies she writes as a staff officer. So I accepted the position.

I suddenly found myself to be a woman in demand. Jim Payne succeeded Turner as brigade commander and wanted me to become his number-two. Then Major General George Goldsmith, commander of the Readiness Command at Fort Jackson, South Carolina, recruited me to become his chief of staff. I no sooner took that job than I was promoted to full colonel in February 2001. I served at the Readiness Command for fifteen months, developing a wonderful friendship with George Goldsmith and his wife, Emmy, that lasts to this day. Major General Goldsmith was my mentor, helping me develop my leadership skills.

I would need a lot of those skills—and perseverance—to get through the next phase of my career. The year 2001 started looking bad in April, over the Easter weekend. I had just finished a business trip to Jackson Hole, Wyoming, and was visiting my mother, who had been hospitalized near her New Jersey home with what seemed like a bad cold. Then a neighbor in Hilton Head got through to me with terrible news: A powerful lightning bolt had struck our Hilton Head home. As a fire inspector later described it, the bolt had actually hit a pine tree in the backyard, raced to the taproot, jumped to the foundation of the house, and climbed through the house to the second floor, where apparently some old paint cans propelled it into a lethal fire. Sixty percent of the house was destroyed. Then just as we were nearly finished rebuilding, our personal catastrophe shrank into insignificance before a much greater one: the terrorist strikes on New York and Washington.

A few months later, I was sent back to St. Pete as commander of the 641st. When I walked into the headquarters, the women hugged

me and grabbed my collar for a look at my colonel's insignia. But we
knew we had a lot of serious work ahead. The 9/11 attacks served as
a powerful reminder of our obligation as a component of the Army.
All the paperwork drills would now be tested. We knew our MP
units would be called, either for homeland defense duty or deployment to Afghanistan. We accelerated our schooling and training
schedules and started mobilizing our units and shipping them out—
one across the bay to provide security for Central Command in
Tampa and for local airports, another to Bosnia to replace a unit
heading for Afghanistan.

I put in a lot of miles flying between my home in Hilton Head
and my command in Florida. One trip in particular would come back
to haunt me. After landing in Tampa one afternoon in October 2002,
I followed my usual routine—throwing my computer bag into the
trunk of my rental car, then going back for my luggage before driving
to my hotel. Only when I stopped at a grocery store for supplies did I
notice that my computer bag was unzipped; while I had left the car
unattended, someone had popped the trunk and stolen my day plan-
ner and wallet. After reporting my loss to the police and American
Express, I went to the post exchange at MacDill Air Force Base to cash
a check. But the clerk would not accept it without my ID card, which
also had been stolen. She suggested that I buy a few items and write
the check for $50 more than their cost.

I took her advice. As I picked up toothpaste, chewing gum and
other minor items, my cell phone rang. I had to pull out a few
things from my bag to get to it. I returned my things to the bag, paid
for my purchases, got my $50 and left the exchange. When a secu-
rity guard approached me and asked me to go into his office, I admitted immediately that I didn't have my ID card. But that wasn't
the problem. He said he had seen me putting something from the
shelf into my bag and singled out my bottle of moisturizer. I told

him it was mine—I always use it on plane rides—and showed him that the bottle was half empty. Nonetheless, he filled out a report and kept the moisturizer. A couple of weeks later, a woman from MacDill's legal office called me and apologized profusely, saying she examined the bottle and recognized that it could not have been stolen from the exchange. So ended one of life's irritating little incidents—or so I thought until years later, when "shoplifting" became one of the Army's charges against me.

At the time, I had many more important matters on my agenda. After only six months in St. Pete, I was transferred again to become the first female chief of staff of the 81st Regional Support Command, which oversees more than 38,000 soldiers. I was mobilized to full-time duty and relocated to the command headquarters in Birmingham, Alabama. We had an important, high-level job, preparing thousands of soldiers, including MPs and specialists in transportation, intelligence, and supply, for mobilization and deployment to Iraq. I will always thank the commander, Major General Michael Mayo, who had worked hard to get me assigned to the job. When Mayo prepared to step down and retire after thirty years of service, I was put in charge of the field ceremony marking the change in command, a real privilege. On the day of the big event, with senior officers arriving from around the country, I decided to skip lunch—food was the last thing on my mind—to go over the critical steps one last time. But I didn't have a choice. I was ordered to go to lunch and found myself seated next to Lieutenant General James Helmly, chief of the Army Reserve. All I could think was: "Why are they doing this to me?"

"Are you ready for the ceremony?" Helmly asked me.

"Yes, sir."

"So what can you tell me that these guys aren't telling me?" he asked.

I'm sitting at a table with all these generals and I'm supposed to start telling the commander about our readiness problems? There was only one answer possible: "Nothing. You got all the briefings."

Maybe he's trying—unsuccessfully—to relax me before the ceremony, I thought. After lunch, I was still trying to clear up last-minute glitches before the big event when an aide came in and said, "Ma'am, General Helmly wants to see you right away."

Not again. "Is anything wrong?" I asked.

"He just told me to come and get you, ma'am."

"Did he look or sound like he was mad?" I probed.

"Ma'am, I really can't say anything," the aide answered.

By the time I got to Helmly, I was feeling extremely harried. "Sir?" I said.

"What's the matter with you, Karpinski," he said. "You don't salute in the presence of a senior officer anymore, . . ." I started to salute. ". . . General?"

"Sir?" I said again. He looked down at the letter in his hands and smiled.

"This is you, isn't it? Janis Karpinski? You've been selected for promotion to brigadier general for command of the 800th MP Brigade."

He looked up at me as he made this statement, and I am certain my mouth was hanging open in disbelief. "Are you serious, sir?" I asked.

He confirmed the news and shook my hand. I was trembling and thought I might just collapse on the floor. The aide, son of a gun, was beaming, pleased that he had not let me in on the surprise.

This news came twenty minutes before I had to lead the biggest change of command ceremony of my life. Now I could hardly walk. I somehow made it through the day. After nearly twenty-five years of practice, I demonstrated that I could march and command a drill while completely flabbergasted. Had I applied for brigadier general?

Yes. Had I expected to get it on my first try? No. And they had given me the 800th MP Brigade—my first choice! My battalion had been subordinate to the 800th, and I had admired the brigade's leaders, always hoping to join their ranks someday. I had punched all the right tickets, taken the tough leadership assignments, and shown dedication through personal hardships—the fire that had almost destroyed my house in Hilton Head, my mother's illness.

Now, in February 2003, the Army was paying me back with the greatest assignment of my career.

The 800th was already deployed, I was told, on station guarding enemy prisoners of war at Camp Bucca, somewhere in southern Iraq. The soldiers were due to rotate back to the States in only a couple of months, and I could wait to meet them here. No way, I said, with memories of Desert Storm, the joys of command and the enticements of the Middle East dancing in my head. Get me an airplane. I'm going to Iraq to join my unit.

•   •   •

I KNEW BEFORE I GOT ON THE PLANE THAT I was flying into a storm. The Army Reserve was stretched thin going into the conflict with Iraq. A surge of volunteers had signed up before the first Gulf war, attracted by patriotism and the opportunity to rake in military pay and benefits for what everybody knew would be a short mobilization. But when many reservists returned home from the war, they had their own version of a post-war letdown. The benefits were not so great after all. The civilian jobs they expected to be waiting for them had disappeared. In many cases, their bases had been closed and units realigned, forcing them to train at locations far from home. As a result of all this, too many officers had gone into inactive status after the war or resigned their commissions. By the time I joined the Regional Support Command in mid-2002, still several months before President Bush approved troop deployments to Iraq, we already were struggling to maintain adequate levels of our Reserve components.

There was tremendous pressure on the generals in charge of readiness to keep those levels up: Their funding and their position in the pecking order correlated very precisely to the number of ready units under their command. Some of them resorted to smoke and mirrors in their quarterly reports to the Pentagon, counting thousands of soldiers who actually were not fit to deploy because of bad health or any number of other reasons. Even massaging the numbers on paper was no easy task. The Army Reserve layered on more and more education and other benefits to attract recruits, a strategy that gave us acceptable numbers but also gave us soldiers who were more committed to the benefits than to the uniform. Some military people complain about the diminishing quality of people joining the Reserves, but I would put it another way: There is a diminishing commitment to a wartime mission among people joining the Reserves. And there is little or no effort to make sure recruits understand that they might have to go to war. As the second Gulf war neared, we quickly observed, volunteers were not rushing to sign up for duty in Afghanistan and Iraq, engagements that promised to be tougher, less certain, and more prolonged than Desert Storm.

In fact, officers and soldiers of every rank were searching for ways to avoid deploying. Suddenly, many officers applied for inactive status, citing personal problems or civilian job conflicts. Many active Reserve soldiers claimed health issues ranging from bad teeth to diabetes or other limitations. Soldiers scheduled for training were not showing up for the courses, rendering them non-deployable. Soldiers were failing to provide plans for child care while they were away, making them non-deployable as well. (Child-care plans had become mandatory after the first Gulf war, when some mobilized single parents and Army couples had abandoned their children, leaving it to the Army to play nursemaid.)

In the best of circumstances, we had to patch together our units to get them ready for combat. Many soldiers designated as members of the same unit had never actually trained together. That was the result of another gesture to reluctant recruits: We had let some of them train at locations closer to their homes while being counted as part of a more distant unit. An MP battalion in Orlando, where the demographics support a large number of MP reservists, might have 200 percent of its listed manpower showing up for training, while a battalion in Tallahassee might have 60 percent, but on paper they were both considered 90 percent full. In many cases, soldiers were not aware that though they trained with Unit A, they actually were assigned to Unit B. Then mobilization orders would arrive, sending them off to war with strangers.

Typically, only one in six called-up reservists would arrive at a mobilization station like Fort Stewart, Georgia, without complications. At the mobilization station you end up with battalion commanders who don't know their brigade commanders, company commanders who don't know their battalion commanders, and soldiers who don't know each other or their leaders at any level. A soldier who grew up in Montana finds herself deploying with a bunch of guys from Brooklyn. A soldier who speaks no Spanish finds himself assigned to a company from Puerto Rico. If the system looks chaotic, it is. At the root of a successful military organization are soldiers who live, train, fight, and survive together. In an ideal 200-soldier reserve unit, 150 of the citizen soldiers would normally come from the same hometown, and all 200 would train and complain—and, if necessary, go to war—together. But most of the Reserve and National Guard units we sent to the Middle East starting in late 2002 had nothing like that level of cohesiveness.

The 800th MP Brigade, which began deploying in January 2003, was no exception. Headquartered in Uniondale, Long Island, the 800th had 3,500 soldiers. But of those, fewer than 500—in the form of the headquarters battalion and one company from New York—had ever worked together. Eight other battalions, along with three fourteen-soldier brigade liaison detachments and separate medical and quartermaster companies, were patched onto the 800th from around the country. Brigadier General Paul Hill, the brigade commander at the time, had the difficult job of piecing together the puzzle, coordinating units that were mobilizing in Maryland, Indiana, and Georgia. Most of the MPs had had some basic training in police duties, including the brigade's mission of running Iraqi prisoner-of-war camps. Exactly how well they were trained and how well they would work together was impossible to say. One key question was leadership: Strong officers and NCOs can pull together a chaotic unit. But here again, Hill had to take what he got for battalion and company commanders, and he did let some problematic leaders deploy. His task was to make it all work somehow. His own career was at stake. Any general who couldn't move a brigade tagged for deployment was certain to lose his job.

The 372nd MP Company, some of whose members would soon become infamous, deployed in April 2003 despite numerous warning signs. The 372nd was attached to the New York brigade from its base in Maryland. Specialist Charles Graner was "cross-leveled" into the Maryland company from Pennsylvania—meaning he was pulled out of his unit and put into another that needed his skill set. At home, he had worked as a prison guard in civilian life, compiling a mediocre record and facing allegations of spousal abuse. With that history, he faced losing the security clearance required of MPs, so his Pennsylvania unit cross-trained him as a mechanic. The 372nd, needing bodies and desperate for a soldier with his experience as a guard, assigned him to an MP position nonetheless.

Graner endeared himself to his new buddies in the 372nd, quickly becoming the company wise guy even though he did not have a leadership ranking. He met Lynndie England and started an affair with her that carried over into Iraq. According to the *Wall Street Journal*, during a night out in Virginia Beach before they deployed, the couple played a trick on a drunken soldier who had passed out. England posed nude with the man while Graner took pictures, an eerie hint of behavior to come. The red flags were flying, but nobody paid any attention as Graner, England, and the rest of the 372nd flew to the Middle East.

My siblings (1964) Top Row: Debby, me, Gail.
Seated: Candy with brother Jay in her lap, and brother Lauris.

My father in his Army uniform.

Airborne Training.
Fort Benning, Georgia.

General Joseph Palastra, Commanding General Forces Command, with me, following Honor Guard ceremony. Fort McPherson, Georgia, 1986.

First all-female Training and Assistance Field Team (TAFT) during a field exercise with the UAE female soldiers during basic training. December 1992.

During a visit to the Kurdish Region, north of the green line, near Irbil, Iraq. From the left: The Executive Officer of the Police Department, The Chief of the Police; me and a Kurd translator. November 2003.

Fatima. One of the first female United Arab Emirates Soldiers. She was a graduate of the first class from Khawla Bint Al Azwar Military School for Women.

Prison camp near Ashref, Iraq. Never occupied. New US construction at a cost of US$ 14 million.

Photo op while seated in one of Saddam's son Uday's gaudy palace chairs.

My husband, George, with me immediately after my promotion to Brigadier General. June 2003.

Heavily looted Abu Ghraib as we first found it, July 2003. Picture of a guard tower in disrepair on the grounds of Abu Ghraib, immediately outside of the area adjacent to the notorious torture chambers.

Visit to Abu Ghraib to review engineer plans in making Abu Ghraib an Interim Facility.

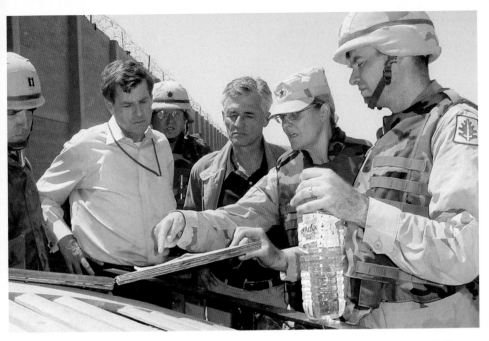

From the left: An Engineer Captain; Ambassador Bremer; Mr. Sergio DiMiello (Chief of the United Nations Mission in Baghdad); me; Major Tony Cavallaro.

A typical Military Police Hummer with equipment, enroute to Baghdad.

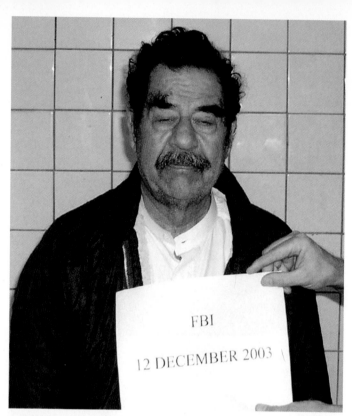

Saddam.
Immediately after capture.

Hallway of Torture Chambers at Abu Ghraib. Used extensively and frequently under Saddam and his sons Uday and Qusay.

THE ROAD TO BAGHDAD

WHEN I FLEW TO KUWAIT TO join the Brigade in June—five months after its first units had arrived—I was giddy with the sensations of being back in the Middle East. Though I arrived long after dark, that familiar blast furnace of dry, desert air hit me as I stepped onto the tarmac. It felt like home. I was back trudging through soft sand under a withering sun, fighting the good fight against the grit digging into my hair, my eyes, my ears, my uniform. The pall of dust in the air told me I was back in that elemental land of adventure and survival, of soldiers and saffron and black ghosts. I took a deep breath and knew I was ready for whatever lay ahead. And in two weeks, I would assume command of the 800th.

Despite my efforts, it had taken me four months after my appointment to get here—putting me on the ground in Kuwait just when some of the first-arriving units expected to be boarding planes to fly home after their six-month assignment. I wanted to be there anyway. It wasn't that I needed my thirty days in the theater, the time it takes to qualify for a combat patch. I had earned my combat patch in the first Gulf war. I just wanted to be in the field with these soldiers, to see them and their commanders fulfilling a wartime mission so that we could build on our successes when we returned back home.

More than the usual bureaucratic obstacles had blocked the way to my deployment. In Birmingham I had received orders to report to Fort Benning to complete my processing. Along with a lot of paperwork, I had to requalify to use the 9mm pistol, the standard firearm for officers (though I preferred the M16 rifle, which is an almost flawless machine). Before reporting, I had a window of opportunity to fly to New Jersey to visit my eighty-six-year-old mother over the Mother's Day weekend. She had been hospitalized again for four days, suffering from a cold she couldn't shake, but I was relieved that the illness had not developed into pneumonia. All of my sisters, brothers, their families, and I enjoyed a pleasant Mother's Day with her, even though her illness forced us to spend it in her hospital room. She was happy.

The next morning I had some free time before my flight and stopped by to see my mother again. When I looked into her room, it was in disarray, with a cart full of instruments pushed close to her bed. I asked a nurse what had happened. She turned and looked at me in dismay, then said, "I am so sorry." She put her arms around me, and I stared at her in disbelief. My mother had just died. Her body lay on the bed, covered by a sheet. She had developed sepsis, a blood infection, and the doctors had been unable to control her fever. In a daze, I called my sisters, brothers, and husband to tell them the inconceivable news. Our mother had died with none of her family by her side. George arrived from his latest training mission, in Oman, just in time for the funeral. We buried her two weeks before I was scheduled to report to Fort Benning for deployment to Iraq.

The Army, always generous in times of personal crisis, gave me the time I needed to help put my family's affairs in order, then I flew back to Birmingham to finish packing out from my old assignment. The command wanted to have a farewell party for me, but I was not in a partying mood. Instead, I suggested to my replacement, Colonel Steve Smith, my friend and running buddy, that we organize a 2-mile run in formation on my last morning, followed by breakfast. We ran to the cadence of jody calls ("You had a good home and you left!" "You're right!"), and headquarters people who hadn't run in ranks since boot camp were whooping it up. At breakfast, fellow soldiers hugged me, consoled me, told me to be careful over there, and I felt worlds better. I told Steve: Next time you throw a farewell party, make sure you run in formation before breakfast.

The flight to Kuwait on a military contract plane was delayed by stop after stop, but military passengers tend to be patient on journeys like that. Any time not spent in theater means you're alive for another minute or another hour. But once I hit the ground, there was no time to waste. I had to inspect my troops, get to know them a bit, and then organize their return to the States. Most of the battalions were stationed at Camp Bucca in Umm Qasr, the facility in southern Iraq where we held Iraqi EPWs. Other MPs from the 800th were conducting confinement operations throughout Iraq, taking prisoners off the hands of the combat divisions and transporting them down to Bucca. Some of our soldiers also were assigned to guard high-value detainees from the Iraqi leadership—the notorious "deck-of-cards" detainees—as well as the camp of Iranian dissidents.

The war was in its mopping-up stage, or so we believed. Bush had approved the U.S. troop deployment in December 2002, launched the invasion—Operation Iraqi Freedom—on March 19, and U.S. forces had occupied Baghdad twenty-one days later. On May 1, the President had declared the end of major combat operations.

My first order of business was to survey our facilities in Iraq. I spent only one day at Camp Arifjan, the modern base built by the

Kuwaiti government to support U.S. troops in their country. Then Hill and I, along with our security detail, put on our Kevlar helmets and our vests and drove off in the 130-degree heat to the war zone. We joined a long desert caravan of lumbering trucks taking troops and supplies into Iraq. Immediately across the border, a trail of shattered concrete structures and skeletons of U.S. tanks marked the coalition's road to Baghdad. Destroyed Iraqi trucks littered the roadside—here a mound of mangled metal, there a little Toyota, stripped of useful parts, flipped over onto its roof. We passed through a broken land of craters, leveled buildings, and markers steering us away from suspected minefields. Smoke hung thick and gray in the air, trapped at ground level during the day by the extreme heat. I sensed feelings of fear from the drivers and soldiers accompanying us.

At Camp Bucca we were greeted by swarms of flies, probably attracted by all that sweating human flesh concentrated in one place. If you stood still for a moment in rainier seasons, we were told, you found every inch of your skin covered by flies. Signs in Arabic and English warned that we were entering a kill zone and would be shot unless authorized to proceed. Eventually we arrived at a by-the-book EPW camp: a series of compounds each designed to hold 500 prisoners, separated by barriers of triple-strand concertina wire and accessible by a central runway. The MPs easily could expand the camp by adding a few more fence posts, concertina wire, and tents—and just as easily take it all apart. Bucca had been operational for four months, so it had all the amenities: portable lights, a mess hall with two air conditioners, some austere shower facilities. But everything about it was impermanent by design. Our war planners assumed or at least hoped that we would need to hold Iraqi prisoners of war for only a few months at most before we would send them home in peace to help rebuild their country.

By the time I got there, the MPs were looking for solid assurances that they would be going home, too. They had begun arriving in January on 179-day mobilization orders. Ordinarily, that meant they should have started going home by now, providing time for physicals and the other demobilization formalities back home. Everything appeared to be on track. After the President declared the end of major combat operations, the MPs had followed procedures for releasing most of the 8,000 EPWs at Camp Bucca. By the time I arrived, about 300 prisoners were left, mostly general officers and foreign fighters who could be set free only by permission of the secretary of defense. The MPs had begun to pack up their own equipment in preparation for returning home.

This was my first chance to meet some of the soldiers in the 800th Brigade, and they looked thin and weary. They did not like the whispers they had been hearing—that their tours in Iraq might be extended to eight months. Their only question was, When are we going home? Some of their questions reflected bitterness. They were concerned about their families, about managing medical coverage for their children and a million other things. Why weren't they being told what was happening? I knew that our mission was expanding: In addition to guarding EPWs, we would have to confine ordinary Iraqi criminals as well, and we would have to send more battalions deeper into Iraq. But I knew no more than they did about our rotation schedule.

"I think you're jumping the gun," I told them. "We have to get some information first, and when it's available—good, bad, or indifferent—I'm going to tell you."

In fact, I later learned that orders already had been cut—while I was still at Fort Benning preparing for my assignment—extending the 800th Brigade's deployment to 365 days and redeploying our headquarters to Iraq. But no one had bothered to tell me, the incoming commander. The information flow and effective communications were already broken.

General Hill and I drove deeper into Iraq, stopping at Tallil Air Base, a trans-shipment point for prisoners being sent to Bucca. The sun continued to beat down, and we noticed tension in the air. At Tallil we took on two additional security teams to deter any Iraqi gunmen who might have tried their luck at taking out two generals, a full colonel, two lieutenant colonels, and a command sergeant major, among other passengers in our group. Our small convoy grew to eight Hummers—six armored and two without armor. The tension increased, as well. The litter of destroyed vehicles and shattered buildings grew thicker the farther north we traveled. Along with the steady line of supply convoys, we saw more soldiers patrolling the roads, and we encountered tanks, armored personnel carriers, and the other heavy equipment that you normally see in combat operations. Turret gunners swiveled their guns and peered through binoculars. Everybody spoke tersely and stayed constantly aware of what was going on around them. The reports we received as we went forward were full of incidents: two Iraqi gunmen killed; small-arms fire; numerous RPG (rocket-propelled grenade) attacks. We avoided anything that would slow us down. If we met a stalled supply convoy, we drove by on the shoulder or in the oncoming lane.

When we stopped to refuel, the sense of danger was almost palpable. As I saw the regular Army troops with all their senses heightened, reacting to any conceivable hint of a threat, it occurred to me for the first time that our Reserve MPs were not seasoned for duty like this. They had all the skills they needed to do their jobs, but did they have the continuous training and survival instincts it would take to guide them through this landscape? I feared they did not.

I had a chance to look into the faces of some of the regular infantrymen. I was a strange sight to them—a female general in battle uniform—and they would often come over to see if I was real and to shake my hand. I would look into the eyes of a nineteen-year-old who looked twelve, wearing his Kevlar helmet and a loaded vest, part of his brain alert to his surroundings at all times. These kids were sitting out there on these roads, protected uncertainly by berms, confident but always watching, trained by diligent NCOs to be always on edge. Reservists sometimes were missing that edge. As I made the rounds of our facilities during the next few months, I pounded home the need to develop a battle rhythm, to wear the Kevlar and vest even if the temperature was well into the 100s. It's easier to identify a body with its head on than with its head blown off, I said—an observation that persuaded many of them to keep their Kevlars on.

After three days on the road, we reached Baghdad. The bustling capital and commercial center now featured stretches of concrete rubble and bleached sand. An unusual odor hung over the city, a blend of burning garbage, dust, and nitrate explosives. Iraqis who ventured into the streets seemed to be wandering around in various degrees of shock. There were few cars on the roads, and the proliferation of coalition checkpoints suggested that anybody not wearing a coalition uniform was viewed as the enemy. It was a terribly disconcerting feeling.

As we made our way around Camp Victory, headquarters of Combined Joint Task Force Seven, I gradually realized that my assumptions about my brigade's future were mistaken. I knew we would have to somewhat expand our role to support CJTF7 from our base in Kuwait. But as General Hill, the man I was to replace, introduced me to staff officers we randomly encountered, I ascertained almost by osmosis that we were expected to shift our brigade headquarters to Baghdad, and that the troops' suspicions were right: Our deployment was indeed going to be extended—how long, nobody seemed willing to say. The soldiers were not going to like this change in plans. When I asked Hill for the details, he would answer vaguely, saying he would show me the orders when we got back to Kuwait. In the meantime, he said, we would spend the next two days scouting locations for our brigade headquarters in Iraq.

This sense of vagueness would torment us throughout our mission in Iraq. When Central Command and other planners decided to expand our mission and send us into Iraq, they should have considered the logistics: What kind of vehicles would we need in the more dangerous environment? How many more personnel would we need for our new responsibilities, and how could we efficiently replace casualties and departing soldiers? Instead, like many other decisions in those tumultuous days, the decision to send us to Iraq was made in a vacuum and on the fly. It was apparently easy for the planners to say, Oh, we need an MP brigade? The 800th is in the area, let's send them.

One intention was to take some of the pressure off the MPs in the regular Army who already were on the ground in Iraq. The 18th Military Police Brigade had provided combat support during the march to Baghdad, performing routine traffic-control missions on the battlefield and rounding up EPWs to turn over to the MP units operating the prison camps. Like all American soldiers, those of the 18th thought the war was over, and that the troops who took Iraq should now go home and turn over operations to the troops assigned to sustain the victory. Instead, when the Iraqi army was disbanded, Iraqi civilians started getting into the act, looting and causing mayhem. They were not yet part of any organized insurgency, just a bunch of hotheads busting through checkpoints and taking potshots at coalition forces. Some would run up to a truck and fire an RPG harmlessly into its side—not realizing that you have to fire an RPG from a distance so that it has time to arm itself before hitting the target. In any case, we were taking a lot of new prisoners, the holding camps in the division areas were already overcrowded, and MPs from the 18th wanted no part of prison-guard duty. Their attitude was: We are combat support; we don't do prisoners.

In the 800th, we did specialize in holding prisoners—prisoners of war, as well as some displaced civilians. But our new orders went far beyond that mission. We were to participate in restoring the entire Iraqi civilian prison system that Saddam had allowed the looters to destroy. We were to help train Iraqi prison guards, but in the meantime we had to operate these prisons ourselves, a mission we had never formally trained for. We knew how to guard prisoners of war, who tend to be docile and obedient, knowing they will be released in a matter of weeks or months. Now we had to guard seasoned robbers, murderers, and rapists, many with no hope of ever being let back onto the streets. This was a much wilier and more dangerous prisoner population. Furthermore, by doctrine we sought to locate our EPW camps in relatively safe, rear areas like Camp Bucca. Now we would have to police prisons amid flying bullets in the heart of a growing insurgency, without the benefit of a dedicated battalion to provide force protection at any of our locations. Did anybody give special thought to training our MPs for this new job? To providing force protection and other special support at the prisons? No time for those details. General Hill was simply given the order to move and had to salute—and now I was inheriting the mission, ready or not. The Baghdad commanders wanted us there yesterday and were already growing impatient.

The 800th MP Brigade is a theater-level asset. That means we plug into a theater command to perform our mission on its behalf—and in return the command provides our logistics, engineering support, force protection, transportation, and anything else we need to survive. In Baghdad, we plugged into CJTF7, but I could sense very quickly that we could expect little support in return. The task force commander, General Sanchez, a short, dour-looking individual, had been in charge only for about a week himself when Hill and I met him in his office. Some commanders, no matter their appearance, radiate dynamic leadership. He did not. The scuttlebutt on Sanchez was that he was focused on his personal ambitions, a three-star general hot in pursuit of a fourth. While stationed in Germany as commander of V Corps, he was so eager to get to the Iraqi battlefield that he moved his Third Armored Division to a port, ready for embarkation, before he had even received the order. His presumptuousness infuriated his superior, the commander of the Coalition Forces Land Component Command in Kuwait.

When we got to his office, Sanchez kept us waiting for a few moments. His attitude said that we were putting him out. We had an appointment, but he was going to make this as brief as possible. He asked us who the senior military police officer in the theater would be. Hill said that would be General Karpinski. Sanchez did not say a word in reply. You can read people's responses even if they're silent, and the message I got was: Over my dead body this female is going to be in charge of all the police operations in this country. He asked me when the change of command would take place—it was June 29—but didn't offer so much as perfunctory congratulations.

That afternoon we visited General Wojdakowski, Sanchez's deputy. He was more than six feet tall and had the upper-body strength of an athlete, reflecting his days as a varsity basketball player at West Point. Hill introduced me, and said I would do the talking since I was about to take command. I started my presentation, saying, "Sir, first off, I'm really pleased to have this opportunity . . ."

Wojdakowski interrupted, turning on Hill, who was a tall, lanky guy himself, a former Special Forces soldier with a very young face;

he looked something like the Shoney's Big Boy. "Well, what's wrong with *you*?" Wojdakowski demanded. "You're still in charge. Why don't you act like a man?"

He bore in. "You're still the commander, right?" he told Hill. "So maintain your responsibility."

Hill was rattled. He always did everything he could to avoid controversy. He stumbled through an ad hoc briefing, mentioning that the next day we would be heading up to Anaconda to scout for a brigade headquarters. Wojdakowski instantly changed his mood—as I would see him do many times later—becoming a sympathetic comrade in arms. He welcomed me warmly, wished me good luck, and commented that I was the only female general he had seen around the camp. He asked me if I was the only female general officer in the theater, and I told him yes, as far as I knew, I was.

When we were dismissed, I had one question for Hill: Where is Anaconda? It turned out to be a major U.S. logistical base in the making about 40 miles north into the outskirts of Iraq's most violent region, the Sunni Triangle. The base's nickname, "Mortaritaville," said it all.

Our drive up there the next day was the most nerve-wracking of any I have ever had in Iraq. After I took what passed for a shower, dumping a bottle of water on my head, we set off through the early morning smoke of Baghdad. Engineers had swept the debris off the road to Anaconda and had built 10-foot protective berms on either side. That didn't stop frequent attacks by terrorists and pirates, so the road also was policed by frequent checkpoints and patrolling military vehicles. Add processions of slow-moving convoys and the result was endless lines and major traffic jams. I was particularly eager not to get stuck behind a fuel truck, imagining the explosion a well-placed RPG would set off. Occasionally an Iraqi head or two would pop up from the other side of a berm. I turned and said to one of my aides, Lieutenant Elvis Mabry, "One or two of those guys could be armed."

"Yes, ma'am," he said, "and they probably are, but they're looking for bigger targets."

That was supposed to reassure me.

As we got closer to Anaconda, where Saddam had once had a major air force training base, I saw a fighter jet sitting in a field. "Is that a MiG?" I asked.

"Yes, ma'am," said Lieutenant Mabry. "Saddam flew them out of Anaconda and put them near farms because he said the coalition wouldn't bomb farms."

We drove past dismal war damage and small fires everywhere. Barefoot kids begging for food or candy came dangerously close to our Hummers. Women trudged along with sacks of grain on their heads or leading a donkey or a cow. Then, almost miraculously, we drove over a rise and beheld a brilliant field of sunflowers spread out before us. I guess there is a heaven, I thought—until I saw a MiG fighter sitting in the middle of all the yellow flowers.

Entering Anaconda, we passed empty hangars and a boneyard of destroyed aircraft. The base was a filthy dust bowl of low, squat buildings. We looked at two or three as possible offices, but they all were too small to accommodate a company, let alone a brigade headquarters. The logistics center itself posed a stunning contrast. When you walked in, you felt as if you had just entered the twenty-first century. Dominating the room was a huge status board and maps that tracked convoys through global positioning satellites. It looked like one of those futuristic command centers that the evil genius in a James Bond movie always hides in some remote place. But outside, it was back to the Middle Ages again. Soldiers living in tents had hung their laundry out where it was getting washed again, this time in dust. Clothes, tents, faces, vehicles, everything was covered with a desert-brown film. One look and I was determined to do whatever was necessary to keep my brigade from moving to this monochromatic nightmare. The living conditions were one thing. Driving back and forth to Baghdad on that explosively dangerous road was something else.

"This is not a good choice," I told Hill.

"Well, if Wojdakowski wants you up here . . ." he said.

"No, no," I said. "You need to tell him this is not a good choice."

And he said, "Well, maybe you could leave just your headquarters down at Victory."

"No, no," I said again. "I'm going to be where the brigade is and the brigade is going to be where I am. Anaconda is not the first choice."

When we went to see Wojdakowski the next day, Hill was hesitant again. "Well," he said, "they showed us a couple of buildings. I think we could work with them . . ."

I cut in. "Sir, it's not a good choice," I said. I told Wojdakowski the road was too dangerous for daily travel and that we had no access to helicopters.

"You don't have any helicopters assigned to the brigade?" Wojdakowski asked.

"No sir, we do not," I said. "We're completely reliant on outside sources for every one of our classes of support."

He turned on Hill again. "Well, why the hell didn't you tell me that?" he demanded.

Hill was in a no-win situation.

After Wojdakowski sent us off to look at possible locations for a headquarters at Camp Victory, I hit Hill with yet another set of questions. Who had decided that we were moving the brigade to Baghdad, and why had nobody told me about it?

"Well, there was discussion about it, and apparently the decision was made," he said.

I wondered if he was being completely candid. To this day I don't know whether he resented my relieving him before he could bring the troops home—or whether he was eager to get home himself and didn't want to hit me with any surprises that might scare me away.

By the time I attended a military police conference in Baghdad a few weeks later, nothing about CJTF7 could surprise me. Colonel Ted Spain, commander of the 18th MP Brigade, took an aw-shucks approach as he lobbied Wojdakowski for an exit date. His wife needed a date so she could help plan a homecoming, he explained. "This is really for the troops," he said. "Can you give me a date to go home, since the 800th MP Brigade is here now?"

Wojdakowski put on his gruff demeanor. "Ted," he said, "everybody is staying for a year." Since the 18th Brigade arrived on February 4, Wojdakowski added, "Three hundred and sixty-five days from the fourth of February means you'll be going home around the third of February." He spoke as if he were explaining something basic to a child.

But this was news to me, too. I got my personnel officer and asked him to find out about this 365 days rule and sure enough, there it was: We had to spend not six months, not eight months, but a full year boots on the ground. My patched-together, under-trained, overextended, poorly supported brigade, now suffering from bad morale as well, was being kept in the firestorm.

THESE ARE *PRISONERS*, JANIS

I MOVED UP TO BAGHDAD BEFORE my superiors had come to terms with the fact that a woman was entering their midst. It turned out that there was one other female general on the ground: Barbara Fast, a one-star, ran the intelligence staff for Sanchez. But I was different. I was commanding troops in a combat zone, and that was a little tough for the combat generals to take. My assignment was doctrinally correct. After all, the President had declared major combat operations over, so it was time for sustainment forces to move in. But everybody knew that my brigade would be setting up in the middle of a hostile fire zone, whether or not you wanted to call it a war. I have to believe that my assignment was an oversight. General Hill was commanding the 800th when the call was made to send us to Baghdad, and whoever made that decision missed the fact that a woman was going to relieve him. Had the planners known, they could have sent the 220th MP Brigade instead; it was assigned to Kuwait, escorting convoys into Iraq, and it was commanded by a man.

But somebody overlooked the little detail about the 800th's new commander, and there I was, once again dealing with warriors who were affronted by my presence. I think some of the division leaders did have genuine concerns about my safety, though they did not express themselves very sympathetically. As our security deteriorated, I heard that some of Sanchez's colleagues started giving him a hard time: You opened the door to a woman, so this is going to be on your head; the next time we go to war and there are female general officers commanding troops, people are going to say Sanchez did that because he let in Karpinski.

Granted, it was hard not to notice me. The troops in the ranks treated me as a novelty, even as something of a celebrity. I never avoided the enlisted soldiers, as some generals did. I liked being around them as I traveled throughout Iraq. I visited their mess halls, shook their hands, and often was asked to pose for pictures with them. I didn't make a big deal of my gender; I wanted them to have a picture of a general officer who was accessible. All I got from Sanchez, on the other hand, was coolness. He showed me as little support as he could at every turn. His attitude permeated the CJTF7 staff: Women want this? They want to be treated as equals? Well, welcome to Baghdad. You made your bed, now lie in it.

My contacts with Sanchez were minimal. I saw him once a week at briefings, and I went to see him separately several times to point out our desperate need for more personnel and for force protection, especially at Abu Ghraib. He visited Abu Ghraib rarely. When he did, he was consistent: He never had a friendly word for me.

But the 800th Military Police Brigade did not require friends or mentoring. We needed the backing of our command. As a Reserve unit attached to CJTF7, our job was to support the headquarters of our military operations in Iraq. In turn, we were totally reliant on CJTF7 for tools we needed to do our job. Maybe in some future war the Army Reserve planners who issue our orders will deploy us only after we have been assured of the transportation, force protection, reinforcements, and facilities we need to fulfill our mission on the ground. But that certainly didn't happen in the Iraq war. In Baghdad, we were put in the position of supplicants entreating our regular Army superiors for favors—and discovering that we ranked very low on their list of worthy charity cases. They just did not see a Reserve military police detention mission as a priority.

I spent a disproportionate amount of time complaining to Wojdakowski and Sanchez that we needed better facilities and equipment and more people. Wojdakowski would say, "Figure it out, Janis," and I would go away steaming. I understood that the staffing levels of military police prison guards could not be the top priority on the CJTF7 commanders' list. The Iraqi insurgency was beginning to take shape and getting hotter. But it was getting hotter for my soldiers, too. Sanchez had tens of thousands of troops at his disposal and could blow his trumpet to summon more whenever he needed them. At a time when our mission was expanding, I was losing a steady stream of MPs through wounds, illnesses, family emergencies, and any number of causes—and I had no such trumpet.

Nor did I have troops trained in protecting us against the growing number of insurgents outside our prison walls. When a mortar attack killed six prisoners and wounded forty-two at Abu Ghraib, Wojdakowski almost shrugged it off. "These are *prisoners,* Janis," he told me. I could understand his point of view: Wojdakowski was a combat officer. But even if you regarded prisoners as expendable, my MPs were still guarding them. I asked Wojdakowski whether I should call my Reserve command in the States to ask for reinforcements. He said, "No, the last thing we need is Reserve general officers involved in this."

"But I'm a Reserve general officer," I said.

"You're here," he said. "You're already part of this headquarters." It was nice to know that I was forgiven for the sin of being a Reserve.

We tried our best to "figure it out." My operations officer, Tony Cavallaro, who should have been insane by that time and, thankfully, was not, brainstormed ways to compensate for our personnel shortages. We consolidated operations where we could. We tried to assign the MPs so that each soldier would have the effectiveness of two. We put guards on fifteen-hour shifts, lengthening their days in order to squeeze more performance out of them. It was unfair and dangerous, but we had no other choice. By the end of a long planning session we would sometimes get giddy. Somebody would propose sneaking out to a motor pool at night and liberating vehicles to transport our guards more efficiently. The problem was that CJTF7 could not spare any drivers. Well, somebody else would suggest, let's kidnap the drivers, too. At that point it would be time for everybody to take a break.

Some of our wild imaginings turned out to be not so inconceivable. A Reserve major in another unit faced a court martial and was sentenced to prison for expropriating trucks to fulfill a mission. We never went so far as to steal equipment—not to my knowledge, anyway. If our scavengers visited a maintenance yard where vehicles had already been cannibalized, our guys might come away with some necessary parts, but never a whole truck. Our warrant officers were logistical magicians who worked out all kinds of deals. Sometimes they would persuade their regular Army contacts to give us replacement parts that the regulars could then reorder for themselves. We had no choice but to work informal deals. Because we were Reserves, we had to go through CJTF7 to order spare parts, and CJTF7 would not supply us because we were Reserves. Sergeant Bilko, welcome to Catch-22.

My logistics guy, Major Bill Green, kept a spread sheet on Hummers, 5-ton trucks, and other vehicles that were approaching their thirty-day limit between pit stops for maintenance. It got to the point where 60 percent of our trucks should have been heading for maintenance or taken off the road entirely. But we had to keep them all running somehow.

The lack of armor on our vehicles became a more critical problem as the insurgency grew increasingly lethal. Even in some of our most dangerous postings, the CJTF7 divisions told us they could not support our travel along main supply routes. I was lucky to have people like Lieutenant Colonel Thomas Cantwell, commander of the 324th Battalion at the Iranian compound and one of the most resourceful and creative people I've met in my life. His soldiers had to drive the hour and a half to Baghdad in soft-sided Hummers with sandbags on the floor—a CJTF7 idea—to deflect blasts from roadside bombs. They took off the useless canvas doors and sat sideways with their seat belts on and their guns at the ready, hoping to shoot the bad guys before the bad guys could shoot them. They would bounce along with their feet on the sandbags and their knees at chin level, just hoping to survive a ride to headquarters. When I think of it now, it's hard to believe what we put our soldiers through simply because of their leaders' lack of preparation.

Sandbags or not, some of our soldiers did lose their legs to the improvised explosive devices (IEDs) along the road. In all, I would estimate that at least twenty-five of our MPs became casualties of our armor deficiencies, including three killed. The insurgents became quite clever at their jobs. Our troops would find an apparently lost U.S. Mail bag—a vital part of any soldier's existence—and it would explode when somebody picked it up. Other IEDs were planted in the carcasses of dogs and sheep. Others were buried along a road, detonated by cell phone as we went by.

Roadside bombs were not the cause of every death. About a

dozen of my soldiers were injured and four killed by mortars and other battlefield encounters. A staff sergeant working in a police station in Baqubah, northeast of Baghdad, approached a box to inspect it and was killed when a terrorist remotely detonated a bomb inside. Two other soldiers died coming off shift when two Iraqis stopped them saying a lady needed help. As they walked up to her car, a man stepped out and shot each soldier in the back of the skull.

Sometimes your luck just ran out. An engineering unit that worked at Abu Ghraib drove out to the prison from Baghdad every morning and drove back every afternoon. On the engineers' very last day, as they drove back to Baghdad in convoy after a tour free of casualties, one of their 5-ton trucks hit an IED under a bridge—always a good, shadowy place for insurgents to plant their bombs. The explosion blew off the rear wheels and killed the kid who was standing in back. Despite the shock of the attack, the convoy had to keep moving. Had the trucks stopped, they would have become a perfect target for an ambush that would have produced many more casualties.

Sometimes, you had no luck at all. One unit newly arrived for duty at Abu Ghraib had no sooner boarded buses at the Baghdad airport headed for the prison grounds when one of the buses hit an IED, blowing a wheel off. They all managed to drive through the attack, as trained. Nobody was injured, but everyone was shaken up. A couple of days later, one of the new teams was transporting prisoners from Abu Ghraib to court in Baghdad when their vehicle hit another IED; two soldiers were injured, hospitalized for a few days, then released back to their units. About three months later, their purple hearts came through. I arranged a ceremony at the Baghdad airport to honor them and another wounded soldier. As they drove to the ceremony, they hit yet another IED. Nobody was injured physically, but I wasn't sure that the two men who already had been hit by three IEDs could even stand in formation. They were understandably shaken up: Their luck just had to be running out.

I talked to them after the formation and gave them an option. They could go back to the States with a unit that was pulling out, or they could stay in Iraq with their present unit. They both insisted that they wanted to stay with their unit, but when it came time for them to get into a Hummer to go back to Abu Ghraib the next day, they couldn't do it. One guy said his legs felt like spaghetti noodles. He couldn't face that Hummer. They spent another sleepless night at the airport, then decided to take the plane. I respected their decision and sent them home with their well-deserved medals.

Toward the end of my assignment, some units started to install jury-rigged armor on their Hummers, but we never put much stock in that. Somebody had found an Iraqi guy who made heavy metal plates and stronger windshield glass to reinforce the soft vehicles. That easily doubled the weight of the Hummers; predictably, they became less maneuverable, their chassis started to break down and their tires blew out.

It would take a lot more than that to improve our safety. We had to get our prisons out of the line of fire. Abu Ghraib was becoming a nightly shooting gallery for anybody who wanted to take a potshot at the American occupiers, yet there were no plans on anybody's drawing board to replace this reviled "interim" facility. At one point, two contractors came out to sell us on "mortar shields" for the prison. They described a material strong enough to deflect ballistic projectiles, something like the nets armored divisions used for protecting their mess tents in the field. In early tests, the developers conceded, exploding mortar shells had produced dime-size holes in the net, but engineers had fixed the problem. I tried to imagine this substance stretched over 60 acres of our prison. "Well, if nothing else it could shade the prisoners in the summer," I told the contractors. What would the incoming mortar shells do, bounce back outside? We didn't need any placebos at Abu Ghraib; we needed real solutions.

At one of our brainstorming sessions, we reasoned that if no-body currently in Baghdad was helping us out, we should look into the possibility of hiring local civilian contractors to improve our facilities. What Iraqi would not jump at the chance to establish a prison-supply company serving all the prisons in Iraq? You could set up a headquarters in Baghdad and employ satellite operations in Mosul, Baqubah, Tikrit, and other major cities where we had prisoners.

When I took the idea to Wojdakowski, he said, "You mean there's not a U.S. company that wants to do this?"

"Sir," I said, "there are a whole bunch of Iraqis who speak the language, know the roads, and would be crazy to get back to work."

"Well," he said, "keep trying to get a U.S. contractor in here."

I didn't want to fight that battle. So I surveyed several American companies, and the representative from MPRI, a firm that specializes in providing outsourced military services, flew over from the States. We met him in Kuwait, and he was very interested in a contract to run the entire Iraqi prison system and train Iraqis to eventually take control. When I told Wojdakowski, he said, "Okay, then do it, Janis."

"Look, it might cost a lot for these guys to come in and do an assessment," I warned.

"I don't care what it costs," he said. "If it's going to fix the problem, do it."

"Okay, sir," I said, jubilant that we finally might be getting some support. I should have been more skeptical.

Next we got in touch with a Canadian company, Sprung Instant Structures, asking if they could provide prefabricated temporary buildings to help us relocate at least some of our prisoners to more secure areas. They had put up cells to relieve prison overcrowding at Rikers Island, in New York, and I thought they might have a solution for us. Once again I went to Wojdakowski and briefed him on the new structures.

"Could they become battalion headquarters?" he asked.

I said, "We need prisons, sir. You get your own company to come over and do battalion headquarters."

"Okay, okay," he said. "I understand. But we might be able to roll up a big contract."

"Sir, I'm not going to give you this information unless you tell me that we can get the prisons done first."

"We'll talk about it when they get here," Wojdakowski said.

"No, sir," I answered. "If we're doing all this work I want an agreement that we'll get a couple of prisons. We need to be the priority here."

He was still noncommittal, but I didn't care; at least he was listening.

Next I had to talk to the civilian prison experts at the Coalition Provisional Authority. I told one senior official about our developing prison deals with MPRI and Sprung Instant Structures, and he simply shook his head. "Absolutely not," he said. "The Justice Department is going to get people over here."

"You know how long I've been hearing that?" I said. But the deal was finished. The Justice Department, which supervised the civilian prison experts, was not going to let anybody tread on its turf, even if we were getting desperate in Baghdad. The prison population was exploding and our manpower was melting away. We needed cells and we needed guards, but the system that was supposed to provide them was, to put it politely, dysfunctional.

THE INCARCERATION COWBOYS

THE JOB OF REVIVING IRAQ'S civilian prison system was supposed to be a partnership. The 800th MP Brigade had orders to supervise and guard the prisons while providing on-the-job training for the Iraqis who eventually were expected to replace us. The job of rebuilding the prison facilities themselves, recruiting the Iraqi guards, and providing their initial training fell to the prisons department of the Coalition Provisional Authority (CPA). Like every other program in those early days of the U.S. occupation, the prisons department was understaffed, overwhelmed, and harried. It needed about seventy experts but had to make do with three, along with a supervisor and a bookkeeper. In the do-it-now, rationalize-it-later atmosphere of the Iraqi reconstruction, the prisons department was under the same pressure I was to "just make it work," without any real plan or guidance. In the civilian world, however, the absence of rules provided opportunities for profit as well as heartburn.

For all the pressures my officers and soldiers faced on their unfamiliar mission in an increasingly hostile setting, none of us ever had to worry about how to account for our spending. Our military accounting procedures held firm whether we were in Long Island or Baghdad. I sometimes had to find innovative ways to finance our needs in Iraq. Somebody had to pay for the basic supplies of the prisons—washbasins, soap, towels, and the like. The infantry commander financed a lot of it in Mosul, and the Brits helped out in Basra, but I had to dig into my commander's emergency relief fund to finance most of the needs for Abu Ghraib and the downtown Baghdad prisons. All of those funds were managed out of the Army, and I had to balance my checkbook, showing an official receipt for every dollar spent, before the Pentagon would reload my account.

The spending rules at the CPA were less stringent. The major contracts on the level of a company like Halliburton rehabilitating the oil industry were handled out of Washington. But all of the local contracting in Iraq—some of it worth millions of dollars—was controlled by the CPA. The hundreds of millions of U.S. dollars seized from Iraqi banks and Saddam's caches all flowed into the CPA offices, where it was used to pay local contracts. There was no bank to hold all that cash; it was simply stored in the CPA finance office. Since there was no bank, there was no one to issue checks making clear who was being paid for what. There was not even a system of official receipts. I asked to see the books in the prisons department once and was amazed at the archaic accounting system. One torn scrap of paper requested $25 for computer and printing support. Another entry ordered payment of $28,000 to an Iraqi prison contractor. Spending for petty cash and for major contracts were all included on the same list, much of it in stubby pencil, many of the bills in Arabic—which, of course, the Americans making the payments could not read. I was never in a position to accuse anybody of financial corruption, but I could see plenty of carefree spending.

The department itself was sputtering along. I had a great deal of respect for its supervisor, Bill Irvine, a ruddy-faced, white-haired Irishman who had had extensive experience restoring prisons in Bosnia, Afghanistan, and in other trouble spots for the United Nations. The three resident civilian experts under his command were something else: the kind of swashbucklers you sometimes see in the wake of a military expedition.

Terry Stewart was the most contentious of them. He got into a pissing match with Bill Irvine that created divisions and bad feelings in the little department. The showdown came at a construction site in Baghdad, where I came upon another of the prison experts, Gary De-Land, engaged in a shouting match with a former Iraqi general who had been brought in to supervise one of the prisons. When Gary grabbed the Iraqi by the shirt, the two men had to be separated. The Iraqi officer explained to me in Arabic that he had been demanding pay for his guards. Gary hadn't understood what the man was saying but was furious that an Iraqi had confronted him. When word of the scuffle got back to Irvine, Bill was even more furious. As he lectured Gary about his behavior, Terry stepped in and said, in effect, you should be defending Gary, not this worthless Iraqi. That was the last straw. Bill fired Terry on the spot.

That left Bill Irvine at odds with the two remaining prisons experts, Gary DeLand and Lane McCotter, both of whom had attracted controversy while serving as head of the Utah Corrections Department. DeLand, who oversaw the department in the 1980s, denied charges by civil-rights lawyers that he had delayed providing medical care to inmates. McCotter, his successor, resigned under pressure after an inmate died in custody; the prisoner had been left strapped to a restraining chair for sixteen hours. In Baghdad, McCotter carried himself in a more professional manner than DeLand, who went about his job like some kind of cowboy commando, with a knife strapped to his leg, a side arm on his belt, and an automatic rifle slung across his back.

Their job was to rehabilitate all seventeen of the civilian prisons we were responsible for throughout Iraq, which often involved costly construction, plumbing, and electrical work. They had to mobilize the resources they needed to show results fast. The best way to do that, of course, was to flash a lot of money. They would bring their receipts to the coalition finance office and come out with thousands of dollars. Handling that much cash could be fun. McCotter and De-Land once had photos taken of themselves holding fists full of U.S. dollars, with more bills sticking out of their pockets. One time they drew $3.1 million to pay for prison contracts. Since there was no bank, they kept the money in an unused bathroom in the prisons department. They had photos taken of themselves sitting on the bricks of cash, which formed a pile about the height of a barbecue grill.

There always seemed to be more where that came from. In one case, the prison experts reported paying a contractor thousands of dollars to install floor tile in a wing of the Kadamiya women's prison, which was being renovated. About a week later, they reported that all of the tile had been looted. So they paid the contractor again to install more tile. Then they said the tiles had disappeared again. So they paid the contractor a third time. In all, the CPA paid more than $65,000 for what should have been no more than a $20,000 job. It wasn't hard for me to imagine the contractor looting and reinstalling his own tiles again and again. McCotter and DeLand asked me to assign MPs to guard their projects, but I refused. I could not spare MPs to guard empty prisons; I would assign our soldiers when they actually had prisoners to guard. (I later relented, and did assign MPs to monitor some construction sites.) It was up to the prison experts to build the costs of civilian guards into their contracts, as other project coordinators were doing.

All the while, McCotter and DeLand gave us progress reports on every prison, often noting delays. If the completion date was September, they would report in August that the project had to be delayed ninety days because the contractor quit, the tiles disappeared, whatever. Every week I had to brief Sanchez and Bremer on our progress, explaining why the 700 new prison beds we had expected still were not available.

At the end of September, McCotter and DeLand left. Their replacements were not due for another forty-five days, so Irvine volunteered himself to supply the progress reports. Soon afterward, he called the operations center, said he had to speak to me and suggested we meet for tea the next morning. I arrived at his office at 6:30, worried about why he wanted to meet so urgently. Had one of our soldiers tried to hang himself or something? He greeted me gravely, full of apologies. Our prison rehabilitation program was in worse shape than any of us had imagined, he said, adding: "I spent the day yesterday going out to look at the facilities, and I see no evidence of any work in any of them."

"Okay," I said, looking for some ray of hope. "At least there's tile in Kadamiya." No, he said. The tile had disappeared for a third time. The contractor had indeed hired a guard for the facility (and the guard, not unusually, had brought his wife to keep him company). But the guard was saying he had never seen tile on that reportedly much-redecorated floor.

I suggested that we visit more facilities the next morning. I knew that *some* work had been done. At Abu Ghraib, where we had a major presence and served as unofficial site supervisors, the Iraqi contractor had showed up diligently with men who worked hard and well, even if their construction methods looked medieval to us. I also had seen real progress at Tasferat and Russafa, twin prisons for adult men in Baghdad.

The next morning we drove off on our tour, and I was quickly deflated. I don't know what a half-million dollars' worth of work looks like, but I know I didn't see evidence of significant construction under way at most of the five or six prisons we visited that day. Here and there we saw signs of activity—some cement-mixing buckets or trowels lying around—but no actual work had been done. We looked at the first two prisons and said the next one must show some signs of work. But no. Well, then, the next one. No again. Even where work had been completed, the job was inadequate. The prison experts had issued the most general kind of work orders: Restore prisons to operational standards. The orders included none of the detailed specifications you see in any serious government work statement. Put orders like that together with inexperienced contractors, and trouble was unavoidable. At Tasferat and Russafa, we had to reroute electrical lines that had been run down the center of the cellblocks, where prisoners could pull down the wiring to electrocute or hang themselves. We had to bolt down bunk beds that prisoners could have used as weapons against their guards.

We eventually transferred prisoners from Abu Ghraib to Tasferat and Russafa. We put Iraqis who had been through the prison department's eight-hour guard course in charge, with our own MPs staying out of sight in the background. One day an Iraqi guard came running out shouting that there was a problem, a big problem. The U.S. sergeant of the guard rushed in and found all the prisoners milling around outside of their cells, laughing and joking. It turned out that the building contractor had installed the door hinges inside the cells; the prisoners simply had lifted the pins out of the hinges and walked free. The Iraqi guards had fled in panic. Our MPs quickly ordered the prisoners back into their cells and told them not to do that again. Some of the prisoners even helped pin the cell doors back in place. We quickly called in a new contractor to redo the doors.

At another downtown Baghdad jail, we put retrained Iraqi corrections officers on the afternoon shift, again with MPs in the background. The Iraqis did not like working alone, so we assigned them in pairs—two in each guard tower, two at each entry point, two on the food detail, and so on. Late in the day, an American NCO arriving for the night shift stopped by the jail to have a cigarette and later said he had to rub his eyes. Iraqi prisoners simply were climbing out of a window on the side of the facility and running away. The NCO sounded the alarm, and our quick-reaction force rounded up about half of the ten prisoners who had escaped. We later discovered that they had chipped at the concrete around their cell's barred window for several days, then pulled the bars away and slipped out. The two Iraqi guards who were supposed to be watching that part of the jail from a tower had left their posts; they explained that they had grown tired, so they had abandoned their watch and found a cool place to take a nap.

In short, the prison rehabilitation program had become a complete—and very costly—mess. A few days after my tour with Irvine, I briefed Sanchez, telling him that in our estimation, $8 million worth of contracts had been let for work at our seventeen prisons, but only three or four projects had been completed. Sanchez's reaction was predictable. Here was Karpinski again, reporting a problem but not a solution. I was worried he might bill me personally for the $8 million. But instead he turned to his military lawyer and said, "Well, now that this has been dropped in my lap, tell me what I need to do to keep out of trouble."

Nobody ever questioned the prison experts, the contractors, or anyone else involved in the prison building projects. And what if they had? Accountability was so lacking that McCotter and DeLand easily could have blamed the problems on Iraqi contractors, or on me for not providing MP guards to protect their work.

The prisons department was not unique in the way it handled cash. Cash was ladled out just as freely to the contractors who were fixing roads, repairing schools, equipping the police department, and doing many other important jobs. In September, the CPA suddenly froze all funds, and we assumed the auditors were finally on their way. But that wasn't the case. The CPA simply wanted to tally up whatever money was left before turning control of it over to the Iraqis. I was not the only one to suspect that we were trying to hand it to the Iraqis so that any blame for corruption could be deflected away from the Americans. The Iraqis, for their part, refused to take responsibility for the mess the Americans had created and said they would supervise only contracts signed under their watch. After all, they had the patriotic duty of making their country a better place to live, while the Americans were trying to patch the place together quickly—damn the cost—and get out as soon as possible.

ACTIONABLE INTELLIGENCE

AS A MATTER OF NECESSITY, OUR "interim" facility at Abu Ghraib was morphing into our maximum prison for all of Iraq. I kept after the civilian prison experts who were in charge of rehabilitating the facilities. I wouldn't let anybody forget that Abu Ghraib was supposed to be a temporary solution. Have you broken ground on a replacement prison? I would ask. Have you identified a location for this new facility? Sergio Vieira de Mello, head of the UN mission in Iraq, had said a new prison must be ready to replace Abu Ghraib in a year. But de Mello had been killed, and no such modern new facility was in the works.

We did our best to marginalize the old hellhole. While we rehabilitated Abu Ghraib in stages, starting with cellblocks 1A and 1B, we kept most of our Iraqi inmates in compounds of tents organized like the prisoner-of-war camps my MPs knew how to run. Our goal was to steadily reduce the size of this tent city, sending the common criminals—starting with the hard-core offenders—out of the desert heat to indoor prison cells at Abu Ghraib and elsewhere as soon as the facilities were ready for occupancy.

At first, all seemed to be going well. We started to draw down our biggest facility at Abu Ghraib, Camp Ganci (named, like all of our camps, for a policeman or fireman affiliated with the 800th who had died on 9/11). We gave the shift supervisor three lists of numbered prisoners. He read the first list of about forty numbers and ordered the prisoners onto a bus. Then he told them they were going home, released for time served. The bus shook with cheers. He filled up another bus, made the same announcement, and the celebration began again. Then he ordered a smaller group onto a third bus—and broke the news that they were to be moved inside Abu Ghraib. This time the prisoners wailed in grief; they were nearly suicidal. To an Iraqi, moving inside the corridors of Abu Ghraib meant a slow death by torture.

It didn't take them long to see that the new Iraq had different standards. In August 2003, when the first prisoners stepped into the first eight cellblocks we had repaired at Abu Ghraib, they found cells limited to a manageable twelve inmates—a number that was well within their designed capacity and far less than the 100 that Saddam's agents would cram into each cell. Now the prisoners had decent bunks with mattresses, washbasins, towels, running water, toilets, and showers. We treated prisoners with respect and permitted family members to visit. When we started to release some of these prisoners two weeks later—and I saw this with my own eyes—some of them didn't want to go: They had it better in prison than they did at home. Even the infamous MREs, the meals ready to eat that our soldiers got so tired of in the field, became a popular currency at Abu Ghraib. When we signed a meal contract and began serving lamb, beans, and other local food, many prisoners wanted their MREs back. They had formed a brisk market in the little packages of Skittles, apple sauce, and other treats that came with the meals.

In short, Abu Ghraib was working well. Perhaps too well. Within a month after we incarcerated our first prisoners there, the leader of the military intelligence (MI) brigade working at the prison, Colonel Thomas Pappas, came to see me. His MI specialists were in charge of interrogating security detainees, prisoners held because they might have useful information on the anti-American insurgency or on global terrorism for CJTF7 and the Coalition Provisional Authority. We held relatively few security detainees at the time, but they were among our most sensitive prisoners, so we kept them in our maximum-security cellblocks, 1A and 1B. Pappas had asked the civilian prisons department to let him take control of 1A solely for his security detainees, and had been turned down flat. Now he asked me to intercede. I recognized that most of the prisoners in the hard cells were indeed security detainees, so I visited Lane McCotter at the prisons department and endorsed Pappas's request. McCotter reluctantly conceded. "I'll go along because you're asking me," he said, "but all of a sudden we're going to have a run of bank robberies and where are you going to put the robbers?" I pointed out that we didn't have to worry about that scenario: None of Iraq's financial institutions was functioning at that point; there were no banks to rob.

McCotter had another warning for me: "You watch. They're going to ask for more."

I reserved judgment, but he was right. Before two weeks had passed, Pappas was back, this time asking for 1B. He didn't want merely the use of the cells, he wanted to take charge of 1A for adult male security detainees and 1B for female and adolescent detainees.

"Then you don't need my MPs anymore?" I asked him.

"No, no, ma'am," he said, correcting me instantly. "We need the MPs because they're going to be feeding the prisoners and accounting for them and signing them out when the interrogators need them."

I said, "Well, the MPs are already doing that. So if that's what you need them to do, they'll continue to do that."

In retrospect, it is clear now that we let the chain of command become too muddled. The civilian prisons people were in charge of the infrastructure because they built it, my brigade was in charge of guarding the prisoners, and now military intelligence was claiming control over the most sensitive of these. We should at least have drawn up a memorandum carefully delineating the responsibilities of the various parties involved, but we did not. At the time, our plan for Abu Ghraib seemed to be working well, and our handshake agreements seemed adequate.

After taking control of 1A and 1B, MI needed to make them more secure. Since the cellblocks were located off the entrance to the renovated portion of the prison, Iraqi guards and other employees coming to work could look into the cells and identify our most prized prisoners. So the MI agents installed plywood over the bars in the doors to the cellblocks, and later installed plywood over the windows, as well.

Phillabaum, commander of the MP battalion responsible for the prison, worried that the MPs responsible for guarding the prisoners would not have access to them. "Sure, the Iraqi guards can't see the prisoners, but neither can the shift supervisors," he said, words that have come back to haunt me again and again.

Pappas assured him that the MPs need only knock on the door to gain access to the sensitive cells.

All these little agreements and compromises came at a time when we felt we had a grip on our jobs. Our MPs were managing the prisoners well. Our tent camps were under capacity, and we had begun our program to move prisoners inside. For a brief while in July and early August we achieved something like a routine.

Our soldiers adjusted to the challenge of guarding a tougher prison population. We no longer were dealing with EPWs complaining about a shortage of cigarettes. Many of our charges now were professional criminals. They woke up every morning thinking of ways to get the jump on us and make their escape. With no records to guide us, we could not even effectively identify our biggest adversaries; someone arrested for minor looting might turn out to be a master criminal and escape artist. All we could do was keep our eyes open all the time. On one level, the MPs kept order simply by acting like good Americans, showing everyday concern for the prisoners' well-being. On another, we maintained greater vigilance. We extended our perimeter of guard posts around prison buildings. We also worked to make partners of the Iraqis living in prison neighborhoods. They didn't want these criminals back on the streets any more than we wanted to put them there and often would pass on information about plans for prison disturbances or escape attempts. Our neighbors around Abu Ghraib remained hostile, but to the north, south, and to some extent east of Baghdad, we developed better relations with ordinary Iraqis.

At the same time, Pappas's experts were staying on top of their intelligence mission. His military intelligence brigade stationed three interrogation teams at Abu Ghraib, each consisting of an interrogator, an interpreter, and a recorder. Their job was to debrief the occasional prisoner who had been arrested for a crime but also had some intelligence value. If we discovered that a looter came from Tikrit—Saddam's birthplace—or that he wore a tattoo common to Saddam's fedayeen, we would turn him over to MI for interrogation. In all, only about 10 percent of the prisoners who came to us ended up as security detainees in 1A and 1B, a reasonable case load that added to our sense that we were in control.

That optimism did not last long. Outside our walls, the rumblings were growing louder. Anti-American incidents around Baghdad—at first set off by the hotheads firing a few AK47 rounds here, crashing through a checkpoint there—began to develop into an organized insurgency. More IEDs (improvised explosive devices) appeared along the roads. Mortar attacks on Abu Ghraib became more frequent. In August, a mortar attack killed Pappas's driver and a computer technician. Pappas relocated his headquarters from Camp Victory to the prison complex and began to supervise the interrogations more closely, insisting that his MI specialists get the best information each security detainee had to offer.

Just before that came the windfall that also became our curse. In July, CJTF7 soldiers cornered and killed Saddam's sons, Uday and Qusay. They found lists of supporters that the brothers had kept, and those lists led to a bonanza of information on computer hard drives, databases, and directories. Combat divisions divided up the names and addresses and started a nationwide sweep to round up Saddam's supporters and find the fugitive dictator himself. In their enthusiasm, the soldiers often would arrest entire households, leaving it to the experts to sift out any arrestees with intelligence value. No sooner had Pappas relocated to Abu Ghraib than this tide of security detainees began flooding in. He and his interrogation teams found themselves working frantically to conduct screening interviews.

From my perspective, we suddenly had hundreds of new prisoners to guard and feed. I happened to be at Abu Ghraib on the first night of the raids, when we received thirty-seven prisoners. Interrogation teams worked all night to complete the initial interviews, and the next afternoon one of the MI officers told me that thirty-five of the thirty-seven had no intelligence value and could be released. For me, it wasn't that simple. My clerks had to draw up a formal record of each arrest and forward it to my legal officer and two independent people for review of any possible criminal activity. They would send their recommendation back to me, since I had release authority for criminal suspects. I would usually concur in their recommendation to release a prisoner, but the whole process took two to three weeks—if all went smoothly. Meanwhile, new prisoners kept pouring into Abu Ghraib every day.

And all did not go smoothly. At a briefing in Camp Victory after those first arrests, I routinely mentioned the thirty-five prisoners who had no intelligence value. Wojdakowski, who had been taking notes, looked up. "Don't release anybody," he ordered.

I started to respond, but Wojdakowski interrupted again. "Who told you these thirty-five have no intel value?" he demanded.

"Sir, I got that from the intel people," I said.

Wojdakowski turned to an aide and said flamboyantly: "Get me somebody from J2"—the intelligence staff.

The aide came back with a captain from the intel shop, and Wojdakowski rose from his chair, towering over the guy and pointing his finger at him. "You don't fucking release anybody," he said. "This plan has been put in place and reviewed and you do not release anybody, not of these thirty-five, not any of them they're bringing in."

The captain tried to explain that the detainees had been cleared.

"I don't care," Wojdakowski stormed. "You don't release *any-body*."

After the intel captain left, Wojdakowski sat down, turned to me, and spoke in perfectly normal tones again. "You see, if we release any of them, they're going to go back and talk to their friends, and then all our planning for all these raids falls by the wayside," he said. He had a point. Even if the arrestees were not insurgents, most of them probably had friends or family members who were, and could pass on valuable information about American priorities and strategies.

After that, the floodgates were open wide. In the summer months, we had 700 or 800 prisoners at Abu Ghraib. In September, that number went up to nearly 3,000. Along with the surge of security detainees, the coalition got more aggressive about picking up ordinary street thugs, as well, and sent them our way. The rule around Iraq seemed to be, If in doubt, send 'em out to Abu Ghraib. The Fourth Infantry Division, responsible for Saddam's eastern stronghold, was especially aggressive. Nobody wanted to be accused of releasing one of Saddam Hussein's key henchmen.

Our plan to shift all prisoners from the tents to indoor cells was now in tatters. Ganci had been our main outdoor camp at Abu Ghraib, holding ordinary criminals awaiting cells, and a second, smaller camp called Vigilant held troublemakers and hard-core criminals who needed closer supervision. At first we put the new security detainees in Vigilant, and when it became overwhelmed we expanded Ganci, keeping the security detainees in their own compounds, separate from the common criminals. We continued to try to transfer our ordinary criminals to indoor cells, and the MI interrogators continued to hold detainees with genuine intelligence value in 1A and 1B. But the tent camps expanded steadily, and by mid-October the population in Abu Ghraib's outdoor compounds was overwhelmingly made up of those security detainees who fell in the gray area: We didn't need to keep them, but the MI commander didn't want to release them, either.

The population of Abu Ghraib grew to 7,000 in the fall. (It eventually would rise to about 8,000.) Nobody at CJTF7 paid much attention to our mad scramble to care for them. We needed contracts for food, water, latrines, blankets for the winter months, and on and on. The warriors of the regular Army were used to running small division prison camps where they would hold prisoners for no more than seventy-two days before shipping them out. If the prisoners were dirty, filthy, and stinking, it was of little concern to the warriors, who knew that their charges would be properly cared for when they got to EPW camps like Bucca in the rear. The CJTF7 commanders had created a monster at Abu Ghraib, but they felt no real need to bolster our resources for dealing with these thousands of incarcerated Iraqi citizens, most of them innocent bystanders swept up by the attempts to stop a growing insurgency. As the prison population grew, and as the pressure increased on the interrogators to produce useful intelligence, we could see divergent cultures developing at Abu Ghraib. Our MPs were trained to treat prisoners humanely, because that was the best way to keep order in a prison. MI officers had a different objective: to squeeze as much information as possible out of the security detainees, to obtain "actionable intelligence" whatever the cost.

On two occasions, Pappas, his operations officer, and I inspected other Baghdad facilities that might better serve the security detainees. We found facilities that were secure, harder to reach with mortar attacks, and offered smaller cells, but Pappas turned them down. He thought that dispersing prisoners also would disperse his interrogators, and that the other locations would be hard to protect without additional soldiers.

As the population at Abu Ghraib grew, the mortar attacks became more frequent, and more accurate. After the early attack that killed six prisoners, the next one, about ten days later, killed Pappas's two MI soldiers. Each attack injured dozens of prisoners and soldiers, though we miraculously escaped suffering many fatalities. The best defense against mortars is offense, but we were not equipped to stop the insurgents before they could strike. That was the job of well-equipped combat units, which should have been provided by the armored division in Baghdad. But none of those units ever showed up at Abu Ghraib for a long enough period of time to be effective. Our luck changed when the commander of the 82nd Airborne Division, Major General Charles Swannack, arrived at Abu Ghraib one morning to do an assessment and determine what support he could pro-

vide. He walked the grounds with me and was amazed to learn that
we were out there in such a dangerous location without any force
protection whatsoever.

As I walked back to his helicopter with him, he asked me what
kind of combat platforms, such as armored vehicles, we had on site.
I told him we had none. He asked again, thinking I did not understand his question, and I repeated my answer. He slapped me on the
back and said, "Man, the CG [commanding general, Sanchez] really
fucked you on this one." He added that he would take care of us, and
he did. A platoon of battle-seasoned, regular Army soldiers from the
82nd Airborne Division arrived to provide force protection, running
night patrols and laying ambushes to try to catch the attackers. One
night the 82nd platoon commander had so many soldiers on patrol
that he said he needed a couple of MPs to supplement his emergency reaction force in case one of the patrols came under fire. Sure
enough, a patrol came under mortar fire, and the emergency force
drove out under blackout conditions to help. The 82nd soldiers in the
lead Hummer had night-vision goggles, but our MPs following behind did not. The MPs became disoriented in the darkness and the
dust kicked up by the lead vehicle, and their vehicle went into a
canal. One of the MPs drowned, and an 82nd soldier who jumped in
to rescue him died as well. The death of the airborne soldier had a
disturbing effect on our MPs. If a frontline airborne infantry soldier
could die defending Abu Ghraib, then how could MPs survive? They
felt like sitting ducks waiting for the next attack.

And we were. Even at our operations center in Camp Victory,
security was less than airtight. When we did the shift-change brief
one night, someone left a light on so that one of the briefers could
read his notes. The next thing we knew, a faraway whistle grew into
a crackling shriek followed by a deafening concussion on the patio
outside our headquarters on Gotham Island. That mortar attack

was enough to shake us out of our complacency. We had grown careless. We quickly went back to our old rule and conducted our briefings in total darkness, using penlights to consult our notes.

By November, barrages of mortar shells hit Abu Ghraib an average of five nights a week. Thursday night and Friday were calm, as the insurgents respected the Muslim holy day (although I'm told they attack indiscriminately now, with little regard for holy days). The prison grounds were one big, fat, motionless target. You couldn't see the launch site or hear the shells being fired, usually from a kilometer away, but when you heard the shrill incoming whistle, soldiers would dive for a shelter made of sandbags and the prisoners would just have to duck. Increasing numbers of soldiers and prisoners were showing signs of mental and emotional stress. The mortar rounds would make big craters; sometimes they hit the roof or side of a building and once blew up a generator we used to pump water. We desperately needed the water capacity, but it took us two months to get a new generator. I went to the CJTF7 commanders, and so did my deputy and so did my operations officer, but nobody was listening. Our superiors would say, with absolute nonchalance, Well, just send some trucks down to Kuwait to pick up a new generator and building materials. Once again, I had to answer: We don't have supply trucks! "Figure it out, Janis."

A security breakdown at Abu Ghraib did capture everybody's attention. One day an informer told an MP that an Iraqi guard had smuggled a handgun into cellblock 1A. Our own guards normally did not carry weapons in the cellblocks, but we did have contingency plans. Following our procedures, one MP carrying a shotgun loaded with live ammunition began a cell-by-cell search covered by a second MP, who carried a shotgun loaded with non-lethal rubber pellets. When the lead MP entered a cell to search one uncooperative prisoner, the prisoner pulled a gun from under his pillow and fired from

6 to 8 feet away, hitting the MP in his bulletproof vest and knocking him back. The second MP fired non-lethal rounds, but they failed to stop the prisoner, who pulled off three more rounds, hitting the ceiling. By that time, the first MP had recovered enough to fire two blasts into the prisoner's thighs, the buckshot he used heavy enough to stop the man but not heavy enough to blow his legs off. The prisoner was taken to the hospital for treatment and ultimately returned to cellblock 1A. Criminal investigators later suspected that this prisoner was one of the abuse victims, but those suspicions proved to be unfounded. Much to their credit, the MPs continued to treat him humanely.

Next we had to find the Iraqi guard who smuggled in the weapon. Our snitch could not or would not identify him, so we imprisoned all forty-two Iraqi guards who were working that shift. Sure enough, after twenty-four hours, they turned in the guilty one. He had taken a bribe from the prisoner's family to bring in the gun, hiding it in the hubcap of a vehicle to get it through the checkpoint.

Sanchez called me in to report on the incident, and he was livid. "I hate MPs and I'm tired of this law-enforcement mentality," he fumed. "I want them to shoot first."

I explained that we were investigating the breach and would seal up any cracks in our security.

"I don't care about the investigation," Sanchez said. "I want them to shoot first. If a soldier's being shot at, I want him to turn around and shoot to kill."

That would be a violation of his own rules of engagement in a prison setting, I reminded him. Our guards normally do not even carry guns. Although a prisoner had found a way through our defenses this time, smuggling a firearm into a prison is an extremely rare occurrence. The weapons we had to worry about were the pieces of jagged rock and glass that prisoners in the tents would hide in their bedding. We would make what the guards jokingly called health and welfare inspections of the outside compounds, gathering up the improvised weapons and punishing the offenders by withholding dinner or cigarettes. Sanchez ordered his legal officer to make the change to the rules of engagement, but in the end, Sanchez cooled down and the changes were very minor.

In September, three months after I had arrived, Sanchez called in the Army's provost marshal—its top cop—Major General Donald Ryder, to assess our prison operations. Ryder came over with more than twenty people and told us what we already knew. The 800th MP Brigade was understrength, overextended, badly equipped, and not appropriately trained to handle many of its assigned tasks. Sanchez had asked for the report, but he essentially blew off Ryder's conclusions. We never saw any improvement in our conditions as a result of Ryder's work.

After another month, CJTF7 gave the appearance of modifying the Wojdakowski rule—release nobody—and put together a review and release board for our mushrooming population of security detainees. I sat on the board, but the signature authority for releasing these special prisoners belonged to Barbara Fast, the CJTF7 intelligence officer. We met two or three times a week for hours at a stretch, and a pattern developed. If we reviewed fifty files and came to a consensus to release six or seven detainees, General Fast would always dissent and send a few of the detainees back for more interrogation. We could be considering the case of a simple farmhand who had been swept up by one of the infantry raids, and the MI interrogators would conclude that he wasn't even a danger to his sheep, but Fast would not release him. She was suspicious of the guy's name, perhaps, or simply didn't like the way he looked. She vetoed the release of many others who had been swept up—in one case a taxi driver, in another two men who had been delivering tea and food to a targeted house. Some of these unfortunate souls already had been in detention for two months, so if they had ever known anything of value, it was out of date by now.

Every soldier knows that intelligence is perishable. The MI interrogators were as frustrated as we MPs. In effect, General Fast was refusing to trust their judgment. "Why is she being so difficult?" one of them asked me.

But I always defended her. "She doesn't want to be on the blame line—none of us wants to be blamed for releasing the next Osama bin Laden," I said.

•   •   •

THE AUTUMN CRACKDOWN AT ABU GHRAIB, like our surge of new prisoners, had its roots in the preceding summer. In August, when detainees had started pouring in, Pappas worked his interrogators 24/7. His teams harangued the prisoners, and he in turn was harangued by Sanchez to get better information. The CJTF7 intelligence people apparently never considered the possibility that the prisoners being rounded up actually didn't know anything. As far as I could see, the MI interrogators were using no special techniques. The MPs would escort detainees from their cells and sign them over to the interrogators, who would take them to the interrogation facility. The MI specialists would ask their questions, then bring the detainees back to the cellblock and return them to MP control. The MPs would strip-search them to make sure they hadn't picked up something along the way that could be used as a weapon, then return them to their cells.

We knew we were on Washington's radar screen. A visit from Defense Secretary Donald Rumsfeld in August made that perfectly clear. We had arranged a tour of our renovated cells, but Rumsfeld preferred to stay outside and meet with some of our MPs. Although "actionable intelligence" was one of Rumsfeld's favorite phrases, the aim of his photo op at our facility was merely to mix with ordinary soldiers—never a bad thing.

The next day we greeted another visitor, who really would change our lives. Major General Geoffrey Miller, commander of the terrorist detention center in Guantanamo Bay, Cuba, had been sent to review the MI interrogators' procedures, to do yet another assessment of detention operations, and to suggest improvements. My senior officers and I doubted he would have much to offer. At "Gitmo," as the U.S. naval base there is commonly known, Miller had plenty of MPs and interrogators to control a relatively small prison population in secure, well-supplied facilities. In fact, he had more MPs than detainees. His prisoners, accused terrorists of many nationalities, were not regarded as prisoners of war, and thus were not subject to the restrictions of the Geneva Conventions. Ours were. It was hard to see how Miller could "Gitmo-ize" a chaotic hellhole like Abu Ghraib.

The MI people invited me to the first briefing for Miller, so I showed up to hear his pitch. I could tell from the body language and the tone of the questions in the room that the military intelligence people at Abu Ghraib were not happy to see him. The MI specialists, with their unique training and skills, tend to be proud and a little arrogant. Most of their questions for Miller, a field artillery officer by training, were challenging. We think we're doing the best job these conditions allow for, the intel people said. What would you have us do differently? One said something like, "We're treating prisoners the right way."

That set Miller off. "Look, the first thing you have to do is treat these prisoners like dogs," he said. "If they ever get the idea that they're anything more than dogs, you've lost control of your interrogation." (Miller later denied using these words.)

At Gitmo, he said, a prisoner had to earn favorable treatment. Every time a detainee was moved—even to see a religious leader—he was put in leg-irons, hand-irons, and a belly chain and escorted by two MPs. When suspected terrorists arrived, they were issued orange jumpsuits. When they showed they were willing to behave and cooperate, they were given white jumpsuits, a status symbol that led to more privileges.

At Abu Ghraib, we had trouble getting prison uniforms of any color, and we certainly didn't have time to waste chaining up our prisoners for every move. Were we supposed to chain up the women and adolescent security detainees every time they moved? Miller had not even seen Abu Ghraib at this point.

I decided to speak up. "Sir," I said, "my MPs don't move any prisoners with leg-irons or hand-irons. There's no need to do that. And your situation in Guantanamo Bay is vastly different from our situation in Iraq. We are mortared every night at Abu Ghraib."

"We're going to talk about all that," he said impatiently. In other words: Shut up.

"Sir, you have eight hundred MPs to guard six hundred eighty detainees," I said. "I have fewer than three hundred MPs to guard seven thousand detainees at Abu Ghraib alone."

"We're going to talk about all of that," he insisted. "My budget is one hundred and twenty-five million dollars a year, and I am going to give Colonel Pappas the resources he needs."

Miller spent some time in Iraq passing on intelligence-gathering tips that later blew up on us. For one thing, he gave the MI interrogators the idea of having MPs soften up the detainees between interrogations, though MPs are not authorized to participate in interrogations and are not trained to do so. Shortly after he left, civilian contract interrogators started showing up to help the military interrogators handle the work load. For the most part, they were former military intelligence specialists, and many came with experience gleaned from Bosnia, Afghanistan, and Gitmo. These guys brought in their own tougher methods for getting prisoners to talk. Miller also recommended the teams of dogs that were brought in to help control the Abu Ghraib prisoners, and Sanchez signed a letter authorizing the use of muzzled dogs during interrogations.

In addition to the civilians arriving at Abu Ghraib, newcomers included military intelligence specialists from Afghanistan, where all prisoners were considered potential terrorists and the interrogation rules were looser, or at least more confusing. As reported in the *New York Times,* a confidential military investigation of detainee treatment at the Bagram Collection Point in Afghanistan documented cases of torture and two deaths after the use of beatings and such techniques as chaining detainees from the ceilings of their cells. The study traced some of these same interrogators to Abu Ghraib. In July 2003—less than four months before the photos were taken in cell block 1A—the operations officer who had been in charge at Bagram took charge of detainee interrogations at Abu Ghraib, and began using "remarkably similar" techniques, according to a high-level Army inquiry quoted by the *Times.*

The creeping MI takeover of Abu Ghraib culminated in mid-November, when Sanchez issued a "frago," or fragmentary order—that is, an order that modifies a previously published order. In the case of the 800th Military Police Brigade, the previous order called on us to take control of all Iraqi prisons. Now the frago made one exception: The 205th Military Intelligence Brigade, under Pappas, would take tactical control of Abu Ghraib. "Effective immediately," it read, "Commander 205 MI Brigade assumes responsibility for the Baghdad Confinement Facility (BCCF) and is appointed the FOB [Forward

Operating Base] commander. Units currently at Abu Ghraib (BCCF) are [put under the tactical control of] 205 MI Brigade for 'security of detainees and FOB protection.'" The order came down from CJTF7 without discussion, without advance notice to either Pappas or me. Once again the chain of command was murky. I was still in charge of the MP guards, but from now on the MI commander controlled the life of the place. The ugly old prison had completed its metamorphosis from a criminal penitentiary to an intelligence and interrogation center.

I never learned who ultimately was responsible for these changes. Miller certainly had a lot to do with toughening up the interrogation methods and probably recommended this action to Sanchez's intelligence aide, General Fast. Fast had the CJTF7 operations center cut the frago giving control of the prison to MI. According to some reports, she was embroiled in a turf war with the CIA, which held some of its secret "ghost detainees" at Abu Ghraib. She reportedly had several disputes with the CIA; in one incident, operatives had shown up at Abu Ghraib to deliver a severely beaten Iraqi prisoner, who almost immediately died. In the end, Fast, who was joined at the hip to Sanchez, controlled what went on in the prison. Pappas, commander of the MI brigade at the prison, worked directly for her. And she sent Lieutenant Colonel Steve Jordan, one of her staff people, out to Abu Ghraib specifically to oversee cellblocks 1A and 1B.

Anybody at Camp Victory could see that Sanchez and Fast were putting immense pressure on Pappas to crack down on the detainees and collect more actionable intelligence. And it's reasonable to assume that Sanchez was feeling that pressure from his own superiors. When I visited Abu Ghraib in mid-January to try to discover some of the details of the prisoner-abuse charges, all the key people and evidence had been taken away, but the shift sergeant did point out one item they had left behind. Taped to a column was a photo-copied letter bearing Rumsfeld's signature block that mentioned the Geneva-Hague conventions and the need for "actionable intelli-gence" and that talked of the use of dogs. In those early days, when I had no idea of the scope or seriousness of the scandal, I didn't make much of the letter and didn't bother to copy it. I still have no idea whether Rumsfeld himself signed it. But I recall that to the left of the signature was a terse notation: "Make sure this happens!!"

Miller later got the opportunity to compare life at Gitmo with that at Abu Ghraib more intimately. He succeeded me as commander of the MPs in Iraq, including those at Abu Ghraib, and also was put in charge of the MI soldiers. He came to the job with real assurances of military and political support based on his successful interrogation operations at Gitmo, including close connections with Rumsfeld's deputy secretary of defense for intelligence, Stephen Cambone.

I wish my own connections had extended all the way to Wash-ington—or at least to Camp Victory. During my tour General Sanchez visited Abu Ghraib for the first time in late September, af-ter the drowning death of the 82nd Airborne soldier. That was his first opportunity to see for himself how bad conditions were. The prison was just barely fit for habitation. We lacked running water, and though we pumped out the outdoor latrines twice a day, that did not make them pleasant. Garbage piled up despite our efforts to remove it all daily, and vehicles raised a constant cloud of dust. Liv-ing conditions were terrible for detainees and soldiers alike.

In short, Abu Ghraib was a dismal mess. After the story of the photographs broke, some journalists wrote accounts of demoral-ized soldiers doing their jobs haphazardly while prisoners rioted, fought, and frequently escaped. I saw something quite different—an unflagging effort by our MPs to create order out of chaos. Com-pany commanders and first sergeants set up day rooms and did their best to establish a recreational program with extremely limited funds. Soldiers often sacrificed or divided the bare necessities, such as water and MREs, in a fair and humane attempt to support prisoners who were confined in compounds with only tents for shelter from the hot sun.

I can say this for duty at Abu Ghraib: There was a lot of urgent and useful work to do. When our soldiers landed a rare opportunity for a four-day getaway weekend, most of them declined, reflecting their dedication to the job of helping their units make the prison work. Was there a morale problem? Absolutely. Soldiers assigned to Abu Ghraib thought they might as well have been sent to hell. As reservists, they were at best second-class citizens in the military. Even temporary camps set up for regular-Army soldiers had Internet and international telephone connections for keeping in touch with their families, for example; we had none. But the overwhelming majority of our MPs maintained their military discipline.

Thirty-four prisoners did escape throughout Iraq on our watch, but roughly two-thirds of them were recaptured. Most of the seven who escaped from Abu Ghraib stole away at night, taking advantage of our personnel shortage: We could not put enough watch guards in the perimeter towers. The guards we did post couldn't see every corner of the prison because we lacked enough light sets and the generators to run them. Nonetheless, we were extremely fortunate to experience less than a one percent escape rate throughout our prison system, a record that would compare favorably with most civilian prison systems.

Sanchez took in the chaotic scene at Abu Ghraib, and it got through to him as my words never had. He went back to his headquarters and fired up Wojdakowski to fix the mess.

Wojdakowski called me in and told me CJTF7 had decided to declare Abu Ghraib an "enduring camp." That designation recognized the prison as a long-term operation supporting a significant number of soldiers, and as such it was eligible for more funds to improve its habitability. Our leaders waved their wand, and contractors started showing up like magic to repair buildings, restore the infrastructure, rebuild the hospital, and add other much-needed improvements. The magic wand did not provide the additional people we desperately needed, but it helped start to clean up the place.

In all, it was a positive gesture from Sanchez. Even so, everything about Abu Ghraib seemed destined to go wrong. The arrival of more contractors and their vehicles every day considerably increased our workload at security checkpoints. Even though these soldiers were willing to work extra shifts and cancel days off, the workers themselves had not been adequately vetted, and some of them turned out to be spotters for the insurgents firing mortars at us. We varied our routines and shift changes so that insurgent spies could not identify an ideal time to attack us—a tactic that put even greater strains on our personnel. When I demanded more help from CJTF7, Wojdakowski had a new way to put me off: "We just gave you an enduring camp, Janis."

Within two weeks of the new contractors showing up, the nighttime mortar attacks grew more frequent and more accurate. Instead of hitting randomly, now the rounds were landing next to troop buildings, next to our vehicle lots, right outside the mess hall. We already had hardened all of these sites. Had we not, many more soldiers would have been killed. There is no question that insurgents had infiltrated the contractor crews and helped coordinate the mortar attacks.

We had problems with our detainee population, as well. After Pappas's military intelligence brigade took control of Abu Ghraib in November, he decided to add more military starch to the place.

He required soldiers to salute their superiors and fall into formation every morning, intending that they stay sharp and communicate a sense of discipline to the detainees. The new measures violated established MP procedures: As on a battlefield, soldiers in a prison avoid saluting and other demonstrations of military hierarchy to make it harder for the enemy—or the inmates—to target ranking officers.

The new rules irritated the MPs and made the prisoners nervous, as well. By the time Thanksgiving arrived, tensions were on the boil. A prisoner threw a rock into an adjoining compound and somebody there threw it back. In no time, 1,500 prisoners were throwing rocks and fighting, and before long just about every detainee compound—about 6,500 prisoners—was involved in the general melee. Only one compound, holding about 480 members of Saddam's highly disciplined fedayeen fighters, stayed out of the brawl. Working through compound representatives, the MPs managed to calm down some of the rioters. They opened up with non-lethal rounds on the others, but the rubber bullets had little effect against prisoners dressed for winter in thick coats and sweaters. Phillabaum finally ordered the use of lethal force against about 700 rioters. By the time the smoke cleared, three detainees lay dead.

It didn't help that we had lost our best MP unit a few weeks before the rioting. The 72nd MP Company had completed its year on the ground and was about to head for Kuwait on its way back to the States. We looked around for a replacement and found an undermanned company that had been running a relatively small prison for the Marines and later for the multi-national allies in Ad Diwaniyah, south of Baghdad. The company was already functioning with only 120 soldiers, two-thirds of its normal strength. To make matters worse, one platoon of the company, about twenty soldiers, had to remain temporarily in Ad Diwaniyah as a security detail for the Coalition Provisional Authority. Reluctantly, but with no choice, we ordered the little half-staffed unit from Maryland, the 372nd MP Company, to relocate to Abu Ghraib.

TAKING THE GLOVES OFF

IT'S STILL HARD TO BELIEVE that within a month, the seasoned soldiers of the 372nd MP Company, with a previous deployment to Bosnia under their belts, would perpetrate prisoner abuse at Abu Ghraib that would shock the world, threaten America's standing in the Middle East, and trigger enough investigations to fill a book the size of the Manhattan phone directory.

These young soldiers could not have had an inkling of President Bush's decision to exempt the terrorists of Afghanistan from the Geneva Conventions, permitting the more extreme interrogation techniques that eventually leeched over into Iraq. They could have had no understanding of the conflicting and confusing rules for interrogation issued at various times, approved by White House legal counsel Alberto Gonzales (now attorney general) and implemented by Secretary Rumsfeld. They had no part in General Miller's mission to "Gitmo-ize" Abu Ghraib, introducing a tougher style of questioning. They had not studied Arab psychology, giving them the tools to humiliate security detainees without physically harming the great majority of them. While it's true that the 372nd MP Company was a patchwork outfit suffering like many Reserve units from the ills of cross-leveling, sloppy training, and spotty leadership, the soldiers had demonstrated one consistent trait throughout their seven months of service in Iraq: They did as they were told. They had orders to confine Iraqi criminals under established procedures at Ad Diwaniyah, and they did so, with never a hint of abuse. For the rest of my days I will believe that, at Abu Ghraib, these soldiers also were following orders when they humiliated and abused detainees.

It was their bad luck to be sent to Abu Ghraib, regarded throughout Iraq as the worst MP assignment possible. But the 372nd was the unit best equipped for the job. Its soldiers had experience in detention, understood all the rules of Geneva-Hague, and were winding down their operations in Ad Diwaniyah. Like most new arrivals, many of them doubtless felt afraid and overwhelmed. Their battalion leaders met them on their arrival, but on a visit to Abu Ghraib I met some of them myself, and I could sense their fear. I told them that in spite of how the situation appeared, conditions were a lot better than they had been a few months earlier.

And they were. But in many ways, the lifestyle at Abu Ghraib was worse than that of the warriors in the field. The regular Army divisions had plenty of force protection and ample water for swimming pools and showers. Such luxuries were unheard of at Abu Ghraib. We had no running water and had to ration what we got. The unit supply sergeant eventually brokered a deal for almost one hundred pallets of bottled water, but numerous attempts to bring in running water were unsuccessful. One MP company constructed shower stalls and supplied them with trucked-in water transferred to a bladder and pumped through PVC pipes. But on too many occasions we could not spare the water for even such minor amenities.

From all reports, the 372nd adjusted to this Spartan lifestyle professionally. After a two-week transition, Captain Armstrong, the outgoing commander of the 72nd, gave me a thumbs-up, indicating a successful transfer of authority, and left Iraq for Kuwait. The replacement troops came in apprehensively, asked a million questions, then quickly developed confidence. Of course, the 372nd was stretched thin when it got to us, and we stretched it even thinner. Its new headquarters, the 320th MP Battalion, did assign soldiers from other companies to help out the 372nd soldiers, but we still had to lengthen their shifts from eight to ten hours and finally to twelve hours, six or seven days a week. Mortars were raining down from outside; inside the prison, frustrated security detainees were demanding to know why they had been arrested, why they could not see lawyers, and when they would be released. There was one bright spot. The 372nd MPs had only five months to go before their own rotation out of Iraq. They were short-timers. They just had to hang in there for a little while longer.

Their time didn't run out fast enough. In early November, at almost precisely the time the 372nd MP Company assumed its guard duties in cellblocks 1A and 1B and elsewhere, more and more American civilians started showing up at Abu Ghraib. These turned out to be the bulk of the contract interrogators who had begun arriving after Miller's summertime visit. Within days after the civilian contractors showed up, less than two weeks after the 372nd began work, most of the prison-abuse cases developed, coincidentally or not. When I was first shown the photos two months later, I was told that seven enlisted soldiers in the 372nd had been identified as participants and that most of the pictures had been taken in early November; some of the date stamps indicated November 10 or 12. My first reaction was: no way. Immediately after taking a dangerous new mission supervising a burgeoning prison population, were we to believe that these soldiers started abusing prisoners on the night shift for their own enjoyment? That's not how soldiers behave, even the bad ones.

The most sadistic troublemaker would have taken time to figure out his surroundings, gauge his supervisors, and size up his colleagues before starting on his so-called "fun."

Take a guy like Specialist Charles Graner, the former civilian prison guard who came to the military with a record of violence against prisoners as well as allegations of spousal abuse. He allegedly served as a ringleader of the cellblock 1A night crew and was one of the soldiers convicted of prisoner abuse. For all of his faults, Graner was not stupid. During his service in Iraq before Abu Ghraib, he was regarded as a can-do leader—the kind of wise guy who takes pride in handling the tough jobs. Graner responded very well to any opportunity to attract attention. But he would not simply have walked into Abu Ghraib and started abusing prisoners as he never had done at Ad Diwaniyah. Not that he would have been kind to them. He was fully capable of treating prisoners roughly, showing them who was boss in his particular way; in one incident at Abu Ghraib, he hit a prisoner so hard that the man almost died. But the kind of cultural abuse that showed up at Abu Ghraib was way beyond Graner's vocabulary.

I can only speculate about what might have happened. The convergence of the new MPs with the civilian intelligence "pros" must have lit the fuse of ultimate stupidity. The MPs of the 372nd found themselves supervising security detainees, the politer term for the "terrorists" apprehended by division soldiers. The 372nd soldiers had never handled terrorists before and must have been influenced by the civilian interrogators, who came to the job with a mandate to crack down, and with worlds of experience. The interrogators enlisted the MPs in their cause, a trick imported from Guantanamo. Soldiers who had been trained to treat prisoners reasonably and humanely now heard praise for softening up the interrogation subjects. Good job keeping the lights on all night; good job blasting music incessantly. Good job because they're really talking now.

In the circumstances, it is ironic that the civilian and military intelligence personnel who had a hand in the abuses at Abu Ghraib largely escaped any reckoning, or at least they did in the first eighteen months after the incidents occurred. As I write this, one low-ranking MI specialist has been sentenced to a six-month prison term; others received relatively minor administrative punishments, such as fines and demotions.

No MPs would have known anything about some of the more sophisticated techniques employed by the intelligence specialists. These methods were aimed at Middle Eastern Muslim prisoners in particular: the shame of being seen naked, the shame of having a woman see them without clothes, the humiliation of wearing women's underwear, the fear of dogs. Only the experienced intelligence operatives could have told the MPs to use such techniques, and in somebody like Graner they probably had an enthusiastic disciple. I have always wondered whether someone in military intelligence had identified Graner as a good type to have in cellblock 1A as the interrogations intensified. My suspicions are based on his propensity for being more aggressive, as indicated by his civilian employment record. The military intelligence people would have known this from the paperwork for his security clearance.

Graner enlisted his girlfriend, Lynndie England, whom he knew would readily join in the sexual humiliation. His shift supervisor, Staff Sergeant Ivan Frederick, joined in the macabre fun, and the company's more senior NCOs and officers, who should have seen what was happening, didn't. I was still commanding the prison during the first two weeks of November, and I never had the slightest idea that anything out of the ordinary was happening there. Neither soldiers nor prisoners reported any infractions, raised any concerns, or reported anything out of the ordinary to me.

My own personnel review and any number of reports afterward highlighted the many leadership failures involving the 320th MP Battalion at Abu Ghraib. General Sanchez was criticized for creating a fuzzy chain of command and allowing General Fast and the intelligence operation to take control of Abu Ghraib's operations. But since we never put together a formal agreement to transfer responsibility for the military police to intelligence, I was judged responsible for the MPs who were an integral part of the prison, and Sanchez and subsequent reports criticized me for allowing the leadership problems to fester under my watch. My defense was that I had to play the hand I was dealt. The 800th MP Brigade had been stuck together with bubble gum and bailing wire in order to make it deployable from the States. The brigade was given rewritten orders for a mission it had never anticipated, then it was handed to me just as it marched into a war zone, short of personnel and equipment, and far beyond its normal field of operations.

Yes, there were plenty of leadership failures. Phillabaum, the battalion commander at Abu Ghraib, was still trying to clear up prisoner abuse cases dating from the 320th's earlier mission at Camp Bucca in May 2003 and was having trouble handling the many new pressures at Abu Ghraib. I had sent out officers to help him and given him two weeks of R&R in Kuwait, but he was not bearing up well. He lacked a command sergeant major, the senior NCO who should serve as a commander's link to his enlisted soldiers. Instead, Phillabaum had to make do with an operations sergeant major named Marc Emerson. Though Emerson was a veteran of Korea and Vietnam, he behaved more like a wild animal than a leader. For recreation, he would get up on the guard towers at night and unload a .50-caliber machine gun on any sheep or dogs that came in range, claiming they appeared to be human interlopers—hardly a model of military behavior for troublemakers in the battalion. Captain Donald Reese, company commander of the 372nd, broke into tears when I talked to him after the scandal broke. He insisted that he had known nothing about the abusive behavior of the night shift, and I believed him.

The company's "first shirt," First Sergeant Brian Lipinski, also pleaded ignorance. He had served in the 372nd since he was a private and knew everything about all of the soldiers assigned to his unit, from their families to their personal strengths and weaknesses. The cross-leveled soldiers, like Graner, were a different story. Lipinski had never dealt with anybody quite like Graner. Lipinski guessed that the night-shift MPs in cellblock 1A had been giving in to their fear and anger over the constant mortar attacks. He apologized for letting me down, for letting Captain Reese down. No apology necessary, I responded. At Abu Ghraib, everybody could share the blame for failure.

In retrospect, I have asked myself whether I was tough enough with these subordinates and in my whole approach to leadership at Abu Ghraib. Did I spend too much effort trying to take care of my soldiers and devote too little attention to training and disciplining them? The honest answer is that these soldiers should have been better trained. Sent to Iraq on short notice in the middle of a war, we had tried to muddle through on the skills we already had: maintaining temporary camps and caring for prisoners of war. I should have found some way to better prepare these young MPs for the much tougher challenges of hardened criminals and terrorists against a background of whistling mortar shells. They thoroughly understood their responsibilities under the Geneva-Hague conventions, but only in the context of routine EPW operations. At Abu Ghraib, when intelligence interrogators encouraged them to "soften up" terrorists suspected of plotting against our country, they had no relevant train-

ing to fall back on, no standards for how to both respect prisoners'
rights and "take the gloves off" against terrorists.

I should have anticipated what was coming. Throughout our
months of handling prisoners, we had respectful relations with the
International Committee of the Red Cross (ICRC), which conducted regular inspection visits to our prisons. When the ICRC inspectors complained about bad sewage at one facility or that
prisoners were getting too little exercise at another, we fixed the
problems. In mid-October—before the 372nd arrived on the scene—
the ICRC visited cellblock 1A at Abu Ghraib and found detainees
kept naked in dark, empty cells. A military intelligence officer told
the inspectors that the prisoners would be "drip-fed" their clothing,
bedding, and hygiene articles to the extent they cooperated with interrogators. The ICRC inspectors noted that some prisoners had
been issued women's underwear in an effort to humiliate them.
Some of the CJTF7 officers got a good laugh out of that one. "I told
Colonel Pappas to stop sending those prisoners Victoria's Secret cat-
alogs," one reportedly said.

When I talked to Pappas about these conditions, he told me all
the procedures used in cellblock 1A were approved. Some prisoners
took off their clothing because they were hot, he said, and some as
a protest; in other cases, soldiers removed the clothing because a
detainee might have used it to hang himself. His explanations
sounded reasonable to me. But I should have asked: How are my
MPs being used in cellblock 1A, and do they have appropriate standards of behavior?

Should I have enforced discipline like Sanchez, haranguing subordinates and poking them in the chest? That has never been my
style and never will be. Bullying soldiers, pushing them to give what
they can't give, is counterproductive. My style is to communicate in
an adult way, clearly and reasonably, making sure that subordinates

understand their responsibilities and the consequences of any failure, and that they respond appropriately. If a leader respects the limits of what her soldiers can do, sometimes they *will* accomplish the impossible.

On Christmas day, only a few weeks before all this broke open, I took my command sergeant major and some of my officers out to celebrate the holiday with the troops at the prison. We also were cheering the capture of Saddam in his rat hole near Tikrit on December 13. I happened to see some soldiers clambering into a vehicle and asked them what was up. They said they were on their way to stage a capabilities demonstration. Intel had said the insurgents were going to try to catch us off guard during the holidays, and these guys were going to send a message that we were on our guard and ready to respond to any provocation. I watched from a guard tower as two helicopters swooped in. They were supposed to fly over the prisoner compound to a mark, where troops from a lurp team (that's how we pronounced the acronym for long range reconnaissance platoon) were to rappel down as if responding to an attack. But the first helicopter stopped short, hovering low over the compound, creating a wind that blew down tents, overturned cots, and scattered clothes in the mud.

I was livid. I called Pappas over and demanded to know what his troops thought they were doing. "If they think this is a joke," I said, "then they can hang around and calm the prisoners down. . . . It's my MPs who have to bring it back under control."

"I'll talk to them," Pappas said, adding: "They're really my MPs."

"We can talk about that later," I said, "but right now you better get that worthless lurp team under control."

He said he would. After that, the commander of the team refused to speak to me. Those who saw Pappas and me go toe to toe also started a rumor that he and I were at odds with each other, though that was not true. We were both victims of the impossible command structure our superiors had put in place.

Neither of us knew what had been happening in cellblock 1A. By that time the shocking photos had been taken, though they were still hidden away on discs. The offending soldiers were sharing them with friends and emailing them home. One night, sometime in December, a soldier from the 372nd named Specialist Joseph Darby was sent to drop off a document in cellblock 1A. Anticipating the company's redeployment in April, Darby was putting together a record of the unit's entire service in Iraq, and asked Graner for discs of photos from their tour in Ad Diwaniyah. While in 1A, Darby saw a couple of naked detainees and made a hasty exit. He had a bad feeling about what he saw and told his superior he did not want to go near the cellblock again. Then as he was looking through the pictures Graner had given him, Darby came upon some of the scathing photos. After considering what to do for a few days, he slipped a disc and a note under the door of the criminal investigation field office at Abu Ghraib. When an agent examined it, he was floored. He gave the pictures to the Criminal Investigation Division chief, Colonel Marcello, and the scandal unfolded.

The photos certainly surfaced at an awkward time. I was caught unawares, visiting the remote compound near the Iranian border. General Fast was in Washington to keep watch on the Senate, which was about to confirm her promotion to major general. Sanchez himself was in the hunt for his fourth star and had every reason to steer clear of scandal.

Among other successes in a bleak situation, Sanchez could say that Saddam's capture had happened on his watch. The deposed dictator was in the custody of what we called "OGA"—other government agencies—a catchall description for CIA, FBI, NSA and other civilian agents operating in Iraq. But eventually he had to be held like a prisoner of war, with rights guaranteed by the Geneva Convention. That required the civilians to hand over Saddam to the military—and that turned out to be us at the 800th MP Brigade. There was some thought of keeping him at Abu Ghraib, but the security threat there obviously was immense. Instead we chose a smaller incarceration facility on Baghdad's outskirts, where we were confident we could keep him safe and under wraps.

After weeks of preparation, Saddam was put in our custody on January 18. This was a tumultuous time for me personally, five days after I learned of the abuse photos and five days before my showdown with Sanchez. But I couldn't let my problems distract me from greeting our new prisoner. On moving day, we staged a number of diversions. We hinted that Saddam would be held outside of Iraq, and we even went so far as to escort a Saddam look-alike to a helicopter and take off as if evacuating him. In reality, we had cleared out a 24-room block for our special inmate just outside the capital he once ruled.

The transfer went off without a hitch, but there was still a sense of uneasiness as I entered the holding facility, which was kept well isolated from other prisoners. MPs from the Puerto Rican National Guard stood watch; we had selected a platoon of about thirty of them to provide force protection around the clock. The center of their attention was a windowless, 10-by-12-foot cell lit by fluorescent lights, its cinderblock walls and floor sealed with battleship-gray paint. The cell contained a cot, built low to the floor, with a thin mattress, small pillow and wool blanket. There was also a modest prayer rug on the floor and a simple table holding a bowl of fruit. I entered through a solid iron door flanked by an aide and a menacing-looking security man, prepared for an encounter with Iraq's Hannibal Lechter.

But the instant the inmate looked up at me, I could see that he presented no threat whatsoever. Saddam had the empty, weary look of a broken man. At 5-feet 11-inches, he seemed stooped and somehow smaller than I had expected, wearing a simple shirt, sweat pants and rubber flip-flops. His hair was jet black (though we provided no dye), his neat beard flecked with gray. In all, he had the demeanor of a burned-out accountant trying to show courtesy to one last pushy client.

He was obviously startled to see a woman dressed for combat with a general's star standing before him.

"Are you really a general?" he said. I had trouble understanding his regional accent, but I managed to carry on our conversation in Arabic.

"Yes," I said. "We have these in our Army. The soldiers protecting you are my soldiers."

"No, they are not," he answered.

"Yes, they are," I insisted.

"No, they are Spanish soldiers," he said. "They wear American uniforms while they are here, but they are very tough—they are from Spain."

I let it drop. I told Saddam that I had come to make sure he was being well cared for. Was everything okay?

He looked around at his austere surroundings as if to say: You can answer that question yourself. All things considered, he would rather have been back in his rat hole.

I asked him if he had any requests.

"I would like some fruit," he said.

"You have fruit," I answered, gesturing toward the bowl of apples and oranges on his table.

"I want apricots and bananas," he said. I responded that I would see what I could do.

He also asked if he could exercise every day, even if only by walking for a few minutes. At the time, he was allowed out of his cell only for visits to his outdoor latrine, a blue, plastic portable toilet—without a door—located at the end of a canvas security tunnel just outside the building. Near it stood a rough, wooden shower that Saddam could use twice a week; in addition, we provided basins of water for daily washing.

As we talked, I noticed his Koran, a clean, well-thumbed volume with a deep green cover and gold lettering.

"Your Koran looks used," I said.

"Yes," he smiled. "I've had it for more than a year."

Then he asked: "Do you know the Koran?"

"I do know the Koran," I said, "and I know the *hadith*"—lessons for life based on the sayings of the Prophet.

I told him I had read the entire Koran. That was true. I have always been an observant Christian, but my understanding of Islam has enhanced my spirituality, showing me how God can infuse one's life and will always answer the questions of one who is pious and patient enough to listen.

Saddam's cell included a small lamp for reading the holy book, but he said his eyeglasses were no longer strong enough to decipher the small print, and he asked for a new pair.

After our conversation—our one and only meeting—the OGA people debriefed me on every aspect and took note of all Saddam's requests. They would parcel out these gifts according to how well he cooperated in interrogations. It turned out that they had changed the lenses in his glasses to make them weaker. He would get better lenses if he deserved them.

I later watched Saddam's defiant courtroom statements on television. He could still marshal up enough of the old fire to look good in public—so different from the broken, rather courteous old man living in the gray cell.

• • •

BY JANUARY, IT WAS TIME FOR MOST UNITS of the 800th Military Police Brigade to start heading home after a year of service in the Gulf. The overwhelming majority of our soldiers could hold their heads high after performing the monumentally difficult job of rehabilitating Iraq's civilian prison system. In early February, we formally transferred authority to the two regular Army brigades replacing us. For a time, the newly arrived soldiers overlapped at Abu Ghraib with the remnants of the 372nd MP Company. Investigators were questioning some of the 372nd soldiers and detaining others. The new guys from the regular Army treated the exhausted, demoralized Reserves like lepers, ostracizing them and giving them the most unpleasant jobs at the prison. When the 372nd finally did get out of the hellhole in late March 2004 and went down to Kuwait to pack for home, its soldiers had to take another blow: The Army extended the unit for an additional four months because the growing insurgency in Iraq demanded more soldiers on the ground.

The soldiers from the 372nd went ballistic. Rumors and conspiracy theories swept through their ranks. Some of them thought the Army would keep the scandal quiet by assembling them in a building at Abu Ghraib one last time and blowing it up, blaming their deaths on the insurgents. As they saw it, their best strategy was to get the story out before the Army shut them up once and for all. One soldier sent a CD of photos to his uncle, telling him to pass it on to David Hackworth, a much-decorated retired Army colonel who had made a name for himself as an author and military correspondent for *Newsweek*. The photos eventually ended up in the hands of CBS, which broadcast the story on *60 Minutes II* in late April, just in time to beat a *New Yorker* story by Seymour Hersh. The world was confronted with one of those open wounds of history that just won't heal. Abu Ghraib, Saddam's torture chamber, was now reborn in the global press as Abu Ghraib, playground of American abusers.

No caricature could be more unjust to the thousands of American soldiers who served honorably at Abu Ghraib and turned the prison into a paragon of decent confinement compared with what Saddam left behind. But the questions will always haunt me. What could I have done to stop the abuse before it started? Why did I not see something like this coming? Why did not one subordinate officer or enlisted soldier tell me about what was happening in cellblock 1A?

In part, my own leadership strategy had come back to torment me. In the military, playing politics to advance your career is largely a matter of tapping into the old-boy network, a losing game for me on the face of it. Believe me, I used every connection I could. But essentially, I had to advance my career in a more straightforward way, by taking on the tough challenges and showing that I could compete successfully with my male colleagues. That's the approach that won me my rank and my battle-zone command. When Sanchez started to play me like a trout on a line, I kept telling myself to focus on the job. I would answer any and all critics by demonstrating how well my under-manned, under-trained, under-supported brigade could perform under satanic circumstances. Nobody looking at our accomplishments could doubt my leadership. Even after the scandal broke, my strategy was to condemn the wrongdoers, but to focus public attention on all the good work my soldiers had done.

In retrospect, my approach was hopelessly naïve. Rather than trying to work through my commander's contempt for me and for my reserve soldiers, I could have used the chain of command much more aggressively. I didn't have to take no for an answer so often. After Wojdakowski ordered me not to appeal for more personnel and support from the Reserve Command, I could have appealed anyway, using my connections to reach decision makers in Washington. After Miller, with Sanchez's backing, talked of getting tougher on prisoners, I could have gone straight to their superior, General John Abizaid, commander of the U.S. Central Command. Yes, Abizaid spent most of his time in Tampa, but I could have reached him there or arranged an "accidental" meeting with him during one of his visits to Iraq. (I doubt Sanchez would have allowed me to schedule a meeting directly.)

I could have been more assertive about going outside of my chain of command, as well. In my meetings with Ambassador Bremer I did indicate that Sanchez was more of an obstacle to our performance than a facilitator, but I never really pressed the case. I also tried to cultivate relations with Paul Wolfowitz, the deputy secretary of defense, whom I had briefed on the prospects for women in the Iraqi Army and other matters. But when I tried to call him after the scandal broke, of course the call was never returned.

After Sanchez shoved his admonishment at me, I obeyed his orders to the letter. I expedited a series of tough assessments, recommending that some officers be removed from their posts, others reassigned. When I handed the results to Wojdakowski, he immediately blew me off. "I've got to go to a meeting and I don't have time for this," he told me. "I'll get to it later on." And that was the end of that. I never heard another word about those supposedly urgent assessments (although the military justice process continued to grind on).

All of my career, I had wanted nothing but to serve as a soldier, yet time and again I found myself singled out not as a master parachutist, not as a rising officer, but as a woman. In the crunch, here I was back in that role I could not shake: the woman in a warrior's world. There had to be a prominent sacrificial lamb after Abu Ghraib, and how could I have not seen who it would be?

•   •   •

THE INVESTIGATION INTO MY PERFORM-ance at Abu Ghraib was all denouement. When the curtain went up, everybody could see immediately what the conclusion would be. The chief investigator was Major General Antonio Taguba, a bureaucrat at the Coalition Forces Land Component Command (CFLCC) in Camp Doha, Kuwait. Taguba had paid a courtesy call on Sanchez before starting his hearings. It thus was no surprise to me that Sanchez hardly was mentioned in the Taguba report and I was fingered as the highest-ranking culprit.

Taguba kept me sitting around in Kuwait for two weeks while he questioned other people. When I finally was called before his panel as the last witness at 4:30 on the afternoon of the last hearing, I actually walked into the meeting thinking that he was investigating the origin of the abuse photos. I was escorted into a CFLCC conference room in Camp Doha, where five men sat at a long, polished table under dimmed ceiling lights. I reported to Taguba, whom I never had met before, and sat down. He began by announcing that among other things he was investigating my leadership values—"the command climate, the supervisory presence of the 800th Military Police Brigade chain of command," as he put it. I was taken aback, but I was determined to keep my voice level, to answer his questions frankly and directly. When he later wrote in his report that I had been "extremely emotional" during much of my testimony, he was not reflecting reality; he was merely using code language for his unspoken subtheme: that discipline at Abu Ghraib had deteriorated under the command of an excitable woman who had lost control.

Less than an hour into the nearly four hours of questioning, it became perfectly clear that I was testifying at the pleasure of a kangaroo court. He asked questions clearly aimed at my competence. Even one of his first queries—Whom did you report to?—had no easy answer. I was attached to CJTF7 and should have been rated by Wojdakowski, but he never went through the exercise. Brigadier General Michael J. Diamond, commander of the 377th Theater Support Command in Kuwait, also declined to serve as my rater, and so did Lieutenant General David McKiernan, commander of the Coalition Forces Land Component Command in Kuwait. While CJTF7 commanded our operations, McKiernan's CFLCC supposedly served our administrative needs. But after the Abu Ghraib scandal broke, neither command would claim Karpinski. A rater is responsible for the officer he rates, and by that time nobody wanted to have anything to do with me.

Taguba also wanted to know how I set my priorities. Did I properly communicate my command philosophy? Did I "feel overwhelmed"? Did I provide notices informing prisoners in their own language of their rights under the Geneva conventions? How many times did I get out to see the units? He asked these questions as if he already knew the answers he wanted. "Do you think proper training, supervision, and effective leadership, not just for that battalion, but throughout the entire brigade . . . could have prevented [the abuses]?" he asked at one point. My answer was no. The abuses reflected a strategy used in one cellblock to soften up prisoners for interrogation, not the performance of the thousands of dedicated soldiers in my brigade.

Taguba asked all the questions. The psychiatrist, lawyer, NCO prisons expert, and recorder in the room said nothing, because there was nothing to say. They knew the script as well as I did. Taguba looked starchy and trim amid the comforts of his base in Kuwait. I may have answered some of his specious questions with an arrogant tone, but his arrogance trumped mine. In his eyes, as in Sanchez's, I was a walking, talking, female insult to the tradition of general officers in wartime commands. Let him have his prejudices. I had made a point of wearing my desert combat uniform to the hearing. And I wore that badge of mine, the set of wings with the parachute in the middle and the star on top, denoting master jumper. That badge stands out on any uniform, but on a woman it stood out like a lighthouse, and I wanted Taguba to see it clearly.

While Taguba asked me about the clarity of organization charts and the imperfections of the paper trail, I was fixated on the quiet air conditioner in the conference room, the soft lighting, the comfortable club chairs. What did any of these questions in this setting matter compared to the dark monstrosity my soldiers had had to endure with so little preparation or support? That impossible mess of rubble and raw sewage. The torture instruments and stink of death. The crowded, filthy tension of the prisoner compounds. The crackling shrieks and concussions of mortar shells. The renegade secrets of cellblock 1A. His questions all led to one theme: my shortcomings as a leader. My answers were equally consistent. My Reserve soldiers marched into that mess, made a decent place out of it against all odds, completed their mission, and left with honor, mourning their fallen comrades. Most of us survived. Stick that record up your prejudices.

"Do you shift all this blame [to Sanchez and his aides]?" he asked at one point.

"No . . . I'm not shifting all of anything," I answered. "I'm taking responsibility, but the situation accurately is a shared responsibility. And they failed us, and trying to cover their failures is going to cost the 800th MP Brigade or me."

At another point, Taguba asked whether I felt that my commanders in CJTF7 were "blowing you off."

"Yes, sir," I answered, and later I elaborated. "They did not want to be bothered by me. And were they blowing me off because I was a reservist? Yes. . . . And for a lot of other reasons? Absolutely."

After a long career spent avoiding the caricature of an "emotional" woman, I made sure to keep my voice level throughout the session. Long before it concluded, I saw clearly that I was being set up. But I continued to sit straight in my chair, resting my arms on the sides, and spoke in a deliberately level voice while he sat across from me taking notes.

At the end of the hearing, Taguba ordered the tape shut off and said to me, "This is an extraordinarily difficult situation."

"Yes, sir, I know," I said.

"And I think about the impact this is going to have on my Army," Taguba said. Hearing the echo of Sanchez's rude formulation, I didn't have to wonder where he got that one from.

"You know, sir," I said, "it's my Army, too."

He flashed a look that said he wanted to argue that point, but he didn't. He showed me the door.

I expected bad news from Taguba's report, but I was devastated by his findings that I had not properly trained or monitored my troops and allowed lax discipline. He had not even questioned me about some of the failings he attributed to me. Yet he recommended that I be reprimanded and relieved of command.

Finally, in April, I was done with Taguba and flew home. Eight days later, CBS aired the photos, and all the world learned of our failures at Abu Ghraib. In many of the news reports, mine was the only high-ranking name mentioned. I was the fall guy. I was still on active duty and scheduled to return from leave on May 24. On that very day—a rainy day in New Jersey—I received a phone call from an NBC reporter. He said, "General, I would just like to know if I can get a comment about your relief."

"I don't think that's news," I said. "I haven't been relieved." I was still in command of the 800th MP Brigade.

"I just came from a Pentagon briefing, and they put it out that you had been relieved," he said.

I didn't believe it. Surely, somebody at the Pentagon would have called me. I told the reporter, "Then my comment is: 'It's news to me.'"

After I hung up, I called the general officer management branch and reached a major who worked for General Helmly. Her name was Rhonda Smillie (pronounced "smiley"). "Oh, hi ma'am, what can I do for you?" she said.

After I told her about the NBC call, she said, "Oh, you're kidding!"

"I don't know if that's a good response or a bad response," I said.

"We didn't have a number where we could reach you," she said.

"You have my cell phone number, you have my home phone number, you have my brother's telephone number, and you have my email address," I said. "Where did you try to reach me?"

There was a long pause, then she said, "I think I'd better have the colonel call you."

So this colonel calls me and tells me again that they didn't know how to reach me; apparently dialing my number, as had the NBC reporter, had not occurred to them.

I made some kind of sarcastic response, and he slammed down the phone on me. So I fired off an email to Major Smillie and told her to advise the colonel not to hang up on a general again.

This produced an email from Helmly, snapping at me for snapping at his colonel, but he never contacted me directly.

Thus did my Army career end in a slapstick routine. Technically, I was suspended pending an investigation of my performance in Iraq, but I knew my service was over. I have spent the last months fulfilling my Reserve duties in South Carolina, talking to a lot of lawyers and journalists, taking vacations with George, and preparing for my retirement after more than a quarter century of military service. In quiet moments I recall my sleepless, exhausted nights in the heat of Iraq, so full of anxieties about what *might* happen. I imagined prisoners digging weapons from the floors of their cells and killing my MPs, prisoners pulling out the overhead wiring in their cellblocks and electrocuting themselves, prisoners simply overwhelming our meager forces and disappearing into the night.

As it so often does, it turned out I'd been worried about all the wrong things. How do I pass the nighttime test now? Do I sleep well? The answer is: most of the time.

In my worst nightmares I watch soldiers continuing to march toward a disaster that I can see clearly but am powerless to prevent. The Reserve MP forces heading for Iraq still are stitched together from cross-leveled soldiers into units that lack cohesion and stable leadership. They still are not appropriately trained to supervise security detainees or to achieve the battle rhythm they will need in places like Abu Ghraib. They still are deploying with soft-sided Hummers and other inferior goods, told to seek better equipment from the active-duty components once they reach Iraq. God help them. Under the strains of mobilization, Reserve chief Helmly said in December 2004, the branch "is rapidly degenerating into a 'broken' force." Give him credit for at least stating the obvious.

Taguba told me that his task was to evaluate my "supervisory presence" and my brigade chain of command. As I saw the mission, we soldiers of the 800th MP Brigade played the role of the first firefighters to reach the inferno: We plunged in to fight it with whatever people and resources we had. We made do. We focused on the essentials. If we could bring the situation under control, our successors would have an easier time of it.

We did make it easier for those who took our place. When we marched into Iraq, only one of the seventeen prisons under our authority was functional. When we left, thanks to the determination of my 3,400 soldiers and the hard work of prisons chief Bill Irvine, all seventeen were in service. Supplementing the efforts of the civilian prison experts, my MPs set up and conducted courses for Iraqi guards. Of the 1,500 trainees we put through our system, 600 Iraqis came out qualified to work under new standards of fairness and honesty. We improved living standards for soldiers—and for prisoners, to whom we bequeathed a new medical facility fully staffed, equipped, and operational.

But that does not end our story. Now that I and some of those under me have been judged and found wanting, who evaluates the chain of command going in the other direction? Officers like me, and Sanchez, too, for that matter, do not make policies. We implement them. And when the policies themselves are as confused and contradictory as ours were on the question of prisoner rights and treatment, you have to look up the chain of command as well as down. I have tried to tell the story of Janis Kapinski and the 800th Military Police Brigade, blemishes and all. On the day the rest of the story comes out, on that day of reckoning, I will sleep very well indeed.

AFTERWORD

THE CAST OF U.S. ARMY OFFICERS
who were sucked into the Abu Ghraib tragedy all have left the theater by now. As I write this, Lieutenant General Ricardo Sanchez is still commanding V Corps in Heidelberg, Germany, and he is still awaiting his fourth star. Major General Walter Wojdakowski is head of the Army's infantry training school at Fort Benning. Major General Barbara Fast is commander of the U.S. Army Intelligence Center and Fort Huachuca, Arizona. Major General Antonio Taguba is deputy assistant secretary of defense for reserve affairs. Colonel Thomas Pappas was reprimanded for dereliction of duty at Abu Ghraib and relieved as commander of the 205th Military Intelligence Brigade in Wiesbaden, Germany. Lieutenant Colonel Jerry Phillabaum was removed from the promotion list, effectively ending his career, and has retired. I have lost touch with him.

Abu Ghraib is still a hellhole. A *New York Times* reporter who visited in March 2005 found the place as tense, overcrowded, and dangerous as ever. The prison is populated entirely by security detainees now; military intelligence still is straining to weed out the real terrorists from the innocents, and MPs are still struggling to keep control. "We've got just enough people to do this," Specialist Chris DiModica told the *Times*. "If anyone gets sick, that's it."

The chain of command, so tangled in my time, is now free of kinks. One general stationed at Camp Victory commands the MPs, the MI interrogators, and the Marines who provide the kind of force protection we had so desperately sought in the early days. The Marines have not been able to stop the mortar attacks, which still hit the prison grounds. And in April 2005 it took a company of Marine reinforcements and three Apache attack helicopters to fight off an assault on the prison by as many as sixty well-armed insurgents, who struck from opposite directions with the support of suicide car bombs. Before the attackers were defeated, they had wounded forty-four U.S. soldiers and Marines. If such an attack had come in my day, there is a very good chance that the insurgents would have overrun us and freed all of our prisoners.

The chimera that we employed to comfort ourselves in the early days—that the stinking, treacherous mess at Abu Ghraib would serve only as an "interim" solution until we could build a modern prison—is a funnier joke than ever. For a time, the civilian prison experts planned to build their state-of-the-art facility in the town of Khan Bani Saad northeast of Baghdad. The place was remote and rural, a more difficult working environment for insurgents. There had been a small prison there, and as at Abu Ghraib a more-or-less usable wall already was in place.

Once the Americans started nosing around Khan Bani Saad, however, the attraction began to fade. When the planners came back for a follow-up inspection one day, they discovered a great chunk of the wall missing; local residents had decided to make off with the bricks for their own use before any new security was put in place. The Americans did hire an Iraqi guard, but when they came back a week later he was gone, and so was most of the rest of the wall. A local sheikh announced that the prison occupied his tribal lands, but that he would sell it to the Americans. The Americans paid the agreed price and sent engineers to start plotting and grading the site. But that work stopped after the sheikh moved 300 people into the prison grounds, all of whom demanded American food and subsidies. Then a rival sheikh had to be paid off so that he would not interfere. Finally, the U.S. planners saw the project as the financial sinkhole it was and left Khan Bani Saad for good.

Military justice grinds on. Specialist Charles Graner, the night-shift ringleader photographed grinning beside piles of naked detainees, was sentenced to ten years in prison for his actions. Graner declined to testify at his court-martial, but in a later sworn statement to Army investigators, as reported in the *Washington Times,* he blamed military intelligence for ordering the treatment he served up. "In a phrase, I was to manhandle them and treat them rough," Graner said, according to the newspaper. "If a prisoner was not following your instructions, smack them around a little or use cold water, such as throwing a 1.5-liter bottle of water on them. Use the sandbags as hoods always."

He was told to single out certain detainees, he said. "The prisoners [were] known to me as Taxi Driver, an Iraqi; Smiley, a prisoner from Yemen; and Piggy . . . also a third country national. Yell and scream at the prisoners. In Taxi Driver's case, have him wear the female underclothing on his head. Cuff them in different standing positions when they would not remain standing on their own. And utilize loud music in the middle of the night. With Piggy, I was to use the isolation cell."

Most of the other cases from 1A also have been adjudicated as of May 2005. Staff Sergeant Ivan Frederick, the nominal leader of the night shift, got eight years, Specialist Jeremy Sivits one year, Sergeant Javal Davis six months, and Specialist Sabrina Harman six months.

Specialist Megan Ambuhl was reduced in rank and lost pay. Private First Class Lynndie England still was awaiting a final verdict. England had grown up in a little God-fearing West Virginia town much like the community that produced Jessica Lynch, who became a national celebrity after she survived capture and mistreatment by the Iraqis. England's luck ran the other way. Her home had been a trailer park in Fort Ashby, West Virginia, where she worked at a chicken-processing plant before joining the Army. You either stay in a place like that plucking chickens all your life or you do your best to get the hell out of town. England was trying to get the hell out.

Some Americans look at Lynndie England and say: What did the Army *do* to that little girl? But I don't blame the Army or her exclusively. The Army gave her a very tough job in an overwhelmingly masculine environment. And she responded as other young women have, seeking out men to prove to themselves that they are still women. Some young women, barely out of their teens, attach themselves to a man almost as a father figure—and of course, there are plenty of men who take advantage of that. Now, caring for the son she had by Graner in October 2004, this impoverished, undereducated young woman—she is in her early twenties but looks fourteen—could end up as a prison mom.

Almost by the day, reports and revelations come out demonstrating beyond doubt that the abuses at Abu Ghraib were a small part of the overall picture. Nothing can excuse the outright physical abuse that took place in cellblock 1A: beating a prisoner unconscious, stomping on prisoners' fingers, sodomizing a prisoner with a broom, and all the other outrages. Most of the actual photos of cellblock 1A's gang in action did not show physical torture so much as humiliation, an abominable attempt to break down prisoners' willpower by attacking their cultural and religious weak points. But as Andrew Sullivan pointed out in the *New York Times Book Review,* these styles of abuse and torture turned out not to be unique to Abu Ghraib. "They were everywhere: from Guantanamo Bay to Afghanistan, Baghdad, Basra, Ramadi and Tikrit and, for all we know, in any number of hidden jails affecting 'ghost detainees' kept from the purview of the Red Cross," Sullivan wrote. "They were committed by Marines, the Army, the Military Police, Navy Seals, reservists, Special Forces and on and on. The use of hooding was ubiquitous; the same goes for forced nudity, sexual humiliation and brutal beatings; there are examples of rape and electric shocks. Many of the abuses seem specifically tailored to humiliate Arabs and Muslims, where horror at being exposed in public is a deep cultural artifact."

Some of the techniques that made for such gruesome photos at Abu Ghraib showed up at Guantanamo in July 2002, Pentagon investigators discovered—months before we even invaded Iraq. At Guantanamo, one top al Qaeda suspect was forced to wear a leash and act like a dog, the investigators said, and at other times was ridiculed sexually by women guards. Other prisoners were shackled in awkward positions and taunted as homosexuals in the kinds of tactics later used at Abu Ghraib. Such reports convince me more than ever that the MPs at Abu Ghraib were acting under the instruction of intelligence officers, not as rogue abusers.

My personal sentiments count for little against a ledger like that. I am utterly dismayed at how the last chapter of my military career has played out. During my year of suspended animation after leaving Iraq, the Army inspector general investigated several charges against me without questioning me or even informing me of the specifics of the charges. The IG cleared me of making a material misrepresentation to an investigating officer. That charge apparently originated in the Taguba report's unwarranted claim that I had misrepresented the frequency of my visits to subordinate commands in Iraq. I also was cleared of failure to obey a lawful order. That bogus

charge also may have originated in the Taguba report, which criticized me for not passing disciplinary matters—involving such violations as soldiers negligently discharging firearms—up the chain of
command; no such action for those routine matters was required.

The IG said he did substantiate two charges. One was dereliction
of duty, probably originating in Taguba's finding that I had failed to
distribute standard operating procedures and other communications
throughout my command in a timely manner. (Show me a command that did amid all that chaos.) He tacked on the ridiculous old
claim that I had "shoplifted" my own moisturizer in Florida, a non-
offense for which I was never charged, let alone punished. All the
charges had one common denominator: not one of them had anything to do with the treatment of Iraqi detainees in cellblock 1A of
Abu Ghraib prison. All the same, General Helmly formally relieved
me of command, as I had expected. But President Bush delivered a
blow I had not expected at all—vacating my promotion to general
and demoting me to colonel.

It is immensely difficult to accept these verdicts of dishonor from
my government and, yes, my Army, when I know in my heart that I
do not deserve them. At the same time, I remain immensely proud
of my service. I was made for a life in the military, and I like to think
that my experiences will ease the way for some of the women who
will follow me in that career. When George and I retire this year, we
will have spent between us fifty-five years in service to our country. I
have told my husband, now a colonel in the Special Forces, not to allow my troubles to affect his own Army life. But just as I look forward to a new chapter of consulting, teaching, and writing, George
also is ready to find a new way to serve, perhaps by resuming his career as a teacher, perhaps by starting a new career in nursing. Only
someone with the service ethic of my husband could find a link between Army Special Forces and nursing. Change is good. We are a

couple of New Jerseyans who find ourselves drawn to a new life in the West, one of those American places of new beginnings in wide-open spaces; after you have fallen in love with the Middle East, you need broad vistas in your life.

It has been a long ride since I reached that magical gate in Al-abama—in the foothills of the Appalachians—where I gained entry to the world of those smartly marching soldiers and their awesome tanks. Again and again, my trail led to war and to the Middle East. Perhaps my love of the Army and my love of Arabia are really two aspects of the same spirit. In both cases I was drawn to the sensation of adventure, the sense of inhabiting a special place beyond the imagination of other suburban Americans. And in both arenas I remained an outsider, fascinated by the power of shifting sands that could so swiftly become biting storms.

ACKNOWLEDGMENTS

Thank you God. Thank you always.

Thanks to my sisters' children, Andrew Russell, Billy King, Jonathan Russell, Jeffrey King, and Allison Russell for their inspiration, patience in listening to stories of my adventures and travels around the world, and for providing hope for the future.

Thanks to my late grandmothers, Gram Elsie, Gram Grace; and to my late aunts, Dorothy and Peggy and to the late Ethel E. Karpinski, for showing me the way women succeed, for opening doors before me, and demonstrating patience with my insistence in doing it my way.

Thank you to my one and only Uncle Paul.

Thanks to John (JAK) Karpinski, Sueanne Desher, the late and wonderful Joan Bohrman, Cathy Allen, and Phil Bohrman. Many thanks to their children Anthony, Katie, John, Benjamin, Amanda, Sean, Stacey, and Jason who have been wonderfully supportive.

Special thanks to Steven Strasser for his writing talents and his powerful abilities to make it all make sense.

Thanks to the very Reverend Howard Bryant and the congregation of the First Presbyterian Church in Rahway, NJ for keeping the faith, and making sure I kept mine.

In memory of my friends, Walt Mitchell and late Tom Simon whose lives inspire.

Thanks to Major John Adams and his legal team for the relentless support and dedication to pursuing the truth, restoring me and resolving the false allegations against me one by one.

Thanks to the thousands of Soldiers I've had the distinct privilege of serving with throughout my military career. They serve as an inspiration to me each and every day of my life and I thank each one of them for their dedication and professionalism. Every day of my life was better when a Soldier was part of it.

Personal thanks to Marcus Willey, my bodyguard, and CPT Elvis Mabry, my Aide de Camp, who ensured my survival and safety in Iraq, often placing themselves at great risk in doing so.

I want to acknowledge with great respect, the dedication, professionalism and support of LTC Thomas Cantwell, MAJ (retired) Tony Cavallaro, MAJ Lisa Weidenbush, LTC Jim O'Hare, MAJ Doug Proietto, and the legal noncommissioned officers assigned to my Brigade.

Thanks to the people of Rahway, New Jersey, for reminding me there is no place like home.

Thanks to Peg (the Leg) McFadzen, Jerry and Paula Owens, Chief Poisson, the Jazzman, and John Haddon for their reliable friendship.

Thanks to MAJ Joe Acardi, his wife, the students and police officers of Roselle Park for their friendship, protection, and support. You all rock.

Thanks to Joe Moreno for being my friend in Kuwait and to Anthony Moncayo for his constant encouragement and optimism, and for speaking to me in Latin.

Thanks to the women in the military for continuing to strive for the top, despite the opposition.

Thanks to HD and my friends and neighbors on Hilton Head Island and around the world who provided comfort, protection, and safe harbors.

Thanks to Dr. Ayers and his staff for giving me every reason to smile.

Thanks to Gail Ross, my agent.

Thank you to Ed Pound (especially for leading me to Gail Ross), to Osha Gray Davidson, Josh White, Leon, and Jim for pursuing the details of the truth.

Thanks to Hessa, Latifa, Afra Ali, and the women of the United Arab Emirates who always knew their own capabilities and provided an opportunity for me to show them the way.

Thanks to the countless individuals who must remain anonymous for fear of reprisals for their support and encouragement.

Thank you to the MEK for pursuing justice and a better way of life. Their ideology, although different than mine, serves as an inspiration.

Thanks to the people of the Middle East who understand.

Thank you to Miramax Books for this opportunity and to my editor Peter Guzzardi.

Thanks to the cowards, many at the highest levels of the military, who often served as the inspiration for me to continue to pursue the truth with dogged determination.

In closing, this passage tells it like it is, serves as a reminder of the truth, and represents the Soldiers who are really out there in the fight:

"It is not the critic who counts, nor the man who points how
the strong man stumbled or where the doer of deeds could
have done them better. The credit belongs to the man who is

actually in the arena; whose face is marred by dust and sweat and blood; who strives valiantly . . . who knows the great enthusiasms, the great devotions, and spends himself in a worthy cause; who, at best, knows the triumph of high achievement; and who, at the worst, if he fails, at least fails while daring greatly, so that his place shall never be with those cold and timid souls who know neither victory nor defeat."

Theodore Roosevelt, 1910